A Very Special Adventure

The Illustrated History of the Workers' Educational Association

Mel Doyle

Workers' Educational Association

Published January 2003

© WEA 2003

WE*a*

A CENTURY
OF LEARNING

1903 – 2003

Contents

Foreword
by David Lanch, President, WEA

David Lanch, pictured at the opening of the WEA National Archive at London Metropolitan University in 1998

For 100 years the mission of the WEA has been to take education to those who have been least well served by the mainstream provision of the day. It has also been part of the WEA's ethos to advance education as a lifelong process, essential if people are to be fulfilled as individuals and effective as citizens. Throughout this time a key distinguishing feature of its approach has been to vest a critical level of organisational control in the hands of its members and students. The WEA is the embodiment of education of, for and by the people.

The past century has been one of unprecedented and accelerating change. In order to fulfil its mission the WEA has itself had to change. The educational priorities of 2003 are inevitably not wholly those of 1903. From the beginning the WEA has worked with universities, trade unions and government; partnerships have always been a feature of our approach. Indeed they are now more varied and complex than ever. But the type of provision has been transformed. Again, the structure of Branches, Districts and Committees has always been crucial to our democracy, but our organisation has had to develop in order to meet new challenges.

A Very Special Adventure is arranged thematically. It examines the early years, organisational development, relations with government, students and classes, work with trade unions and the international dimension. What comes across is the Association's ability to re-invent itself without losing its soul, not merely to cope with changing demands but to use them to its advantage. The more I learn about our Association's past, the more certain I become that it has a flourishing future. The WEA really is *A Very Special Adventure*.

David Lanch
President, WEA

One | Birth of a Movement
The Formative Years of the WEA

The WEA came into being in 1903, the energetic offspring of one man's vision and a 2/6d loan from his wife. The man was Albert Mansbridge, a modestly-paid one-time clerk in the tea department of the Co-operative Wholesale Society. Initially called The Association to Promote the Higher Education of Working Men, the organisation was renamed the Workers' Educational Association two years later, partly to avoid offence to the Women's Co-operative Guild.

The 27-year-old Mansbridge was a remarkable man who zealously believed that, through self-help and collective endeavour, working class people could transform themselves spiritually and intellectually. This was the vision that persuaded Frances Mansbridge to part with 2/6d from her housekeeping to help launch the WEA.

Past attempts to create formal organisations aimed at attracting working class support had failed, he believed, because workers had not been given the necessary level of organisational control. University Extension classes had only achieved real purchase in working class communities when their local organisation was in working class hands – through an 'artisan committee' or the local Co-operative Society. Mansbridge later wrote that the Mechanics' Institutes had withered in the 19th century because they were largely the outcome of philanthropic effort rather than "the initiative of the mechanics themselves".

His essential aim was to create an organisation which would stimulate, then coordinate, what he called "all working class efforts of a specifically educational character". To achieve this he judged that a partnership between the working class movement and the Universities was vital.

This young man's strength, energy and commitment – and his genius

In 1902 Mansbridge published 'Co-operation, Trade Unionism and University Extension' in the *University Extension Journal*. It was from this, and subsequent articles by Mansbridge and fellow Co-operator, Robert Halstead, that the detail of the 'idea' of 'The Association to Promote the Higher Education of Working Men' took formal shape in May 1903.

In his *An Adventure in Working Class Education*, written in 1920, he emphasised the partnership between the labour movement and the Universities in quite unambiguous language. "There never was a single occasion," he wrote, "upon which the ideals expressed were not in harmony with the spirit of labour." He continued: "Yet because scholarship is a vital force the fusion of it with the experience of life and labour produced a greater wisdom than could have been the case if scholars had been absent or quiescent."

An Association to Promote the Higher Education of Working Men,

PRIMARILY

BY THE EXTENSION OF UNIVERSITY TEACHING:

ALSO,

(a) **By the assistance of all Working Class efforts of a specifically educational character.**

(b) **By the development of an efficient School Continuation System.**

—∴—

Advisory Council:

The Rev. CANON BARNETT.	A. HEWITT.
W. HENRY BROWN.	BOLTON KING, M.A.
The Very Rev. the DEAN of DURHAM.	F. MADDISON.
	DUNCAN McINNES.
ABEL EVANS.	L. L. PRICE, M.A.
The Rev. Dr. FRY.	WILL STEADMAN, L.C.C.
C. H. GRINLING.	HENRY VIVIAN.
GEORGE HAWKINS, J.P.	W. H. WATKINS,

Executive:

GEORGE ALCOCK (Amalgamated Society of Railway Servants).
S. J. CHAPMAN, M.A. (Professor of Political Economy, Owen's College).
Ald. GEORGE DEW, L.C.C. (Amalgamated Society of Carpenters and Joiners).
ROBERT HALSTEAD (Sec. to the Co-operative Productive Federation, Ltd.).
The Rev. T. J. LAWRENCE, LL.D. (late Fellow of Downing College).
ALBERT MANSBRIDGE (Battersea and Wandsworth Co-operative Society).
J. HOLLAND ROSE, Litt. D. (Christ's College, Cambridge).
The Rev. W. HUDSON SHAW, M.A. (late Fellow of Balliol College).
Two Representatives from the Co-operative Union, Ltd.
Two Representatives from the Trade Union Congress.
One Representative from the Association of Directors of Education.
One Representative from each University Extension Authority.

Hon. Auditor:

T B. BUTTERWORTH (Public Auditor under the Industrial and Provident Societies Act).

Hon. Secretary (pro tem.):

ALBERT MANSBRIDGE,
198, Windsor Road,
Ilford,
Essex.

The Conference held in Oxford on 22 August 1903 was the launch platform of the WEA. Bringing together Co-operators, Extensionists and a smattering of trade union representatives, the meeting adopted a constitution and formally elected Mansbridge as Honorary Secretary

for building alliances – were all vital to the success of the new organisation. He had the right life experience: in 1903 he was an activist in the Co-operative movement and had been a student and a teacher in Co-operative Union classes. He was also a close friend of Charles Gore, Canon of Westminster and later Bishop of Birmingham, who opened important doors into ecclesiastical, academic and political life.

Mansbridge's achievement was to interpret the spirit of the time into something tangible and enduring in what was a period of great ferment. Britain was still an imperial power, its industrial dominance not yet fully challenged. The attitudes and practices of the governing classes were underpinned by confidence in Britain's continuing place in the world, and the pre-ordained social order. Socially and politically however, new challenges to the old order were

The sheer vitality and enthusiasm of the WEA's leading advocates shines through the early years. Mansbridge was 27 in 1903. When Alfred Zimmern participated in the 1907 Oxford Conference he was 28, the age at which William Temple became President of the WEA in 1908. It was a new organisation and led by a new generation. Youth was in the ascendant and anything and everything must have seemed possible. In this 1909 photograph of the WEA's 'Officials', Mansbridge is seated on the left, Temple next to him, and T W Price is standing on the right

emerging – most notably in the growing assertiveness of an independent Labour Movement.

Trade unionism now attracted the unskilled as well as the skilled 'craft' worker. Independent Labour representation in Parliament had been achieved, with the formation of the Labour Representation Committee (soon to become the Labour Party). The Co-operative Societies were deeply rooted in working class communities.

In the Universities, the Church and the political establishment, there was enlightened recognition that political, social and economic reform was morally right and politically necessary. Mansbridge's project, with its emphasis on spiritual and intellectual development, was seen as an appropriate accompaniment to reform.

Mansbridge was elected into office as 'Honorary Secretary, pro tem' by Frances at what he described as "a completely democratic meeting attended by both of us and no one else". A Provisional Committee comprising trade unionists and Co-operative activists quickly followed, all close friends of Mansbridge.

In August 1903 the Oxford Extension Summer Meeting served as the

HARRY BOULTER,
THE SOCIALIST TAILOR,
10 till 8 at 108, City Road, E.C.

Cycling Suits and Costumes a Speciality.

Suits in ALL-WOOL TWEEDS from
35/-

COSTUMES from
50/-

Your own ideas carried out in detail.

PERSONAL ATTENTION.

OWN MATERIALS MADE UP.

Everybody who is Anybody in the London Union a Customer.

From the 1890s to the Second World War the fabric of working class life was an extraordinary tapestry of interconnections. Organisational links at work and in the community extended from social and recreational clubs to service and retail outlets. Harry Boulter's advertisement to 'the London Union' was by no means an unusual marketing ploy

William Temple was elected President of the WEA in 1908. As an undergraduate at Balliol College, he had visited the University Settlements in Bethnal Green and Bermondsey. He was to become arguably the greatest Archbishop of Canterbury of the 20th century

1907 Joint Committee of Oxford and Workpeople. Mactavish is third from the right in the middle row, Zimmern is seated second from the left, Mansbridge is seated second from the right and A L Smith is seated on the far right

Association's launch platform, at a specially convened conference. Overwhelmingly the participants were from the Extension Movement and Co-operative Societies – the latter insisting that the Secretary of the Association should be "a working man who was in touch with the aspirations of his own class". Thus Albert Mansbridge, son of a Gloucester carpenter, formally became Honorary Secretary. In April 1906 the post became full-time and the title changed to General Secretary.

Oxford was critical in achieving public recognition of the WEA. Letter campaigns in the national press were led by 'Oxford men' including William Temple, who became President of the WEA in 1908. Charles Gore raised the reform of the Universities, including working class participation, in the House of Lords. In 1907, at what proved to be a seminal event, a Conference titled Oxford and Working Class Education was held at the University, again taking advantage of the Oxford Extension Summer meeting.

Over 400 delegates attended the Oxford Conference representing some 200, mostly working class, organisations. Sir Robert Morant, Permanent Secretary to the Government's Board of Education, was much impressed by Mansbridge. The Conference called for the appointment of a joint University (Oxford)/WEA Committee which was subsequently formed. It reported in 1908, recommending a permanent Joint Committee with equal representation, its own officers and funds and independent from Oxford's Extension Delegacy. It was this report that led directly to the establishment and sustained development of tutorial class provision specifically designed to attract working class adults.

It also paved the way for the first financial support from central government. From 1906 a Liberal Government was in office, and it proved broadly sympathetic to Mansbridge's project and open to the views of the Oxford 'liberal enlightenment'. The basis for future public funding was established – a mix of central and local government grant, University support, affiliation and course fees

Albert Mansbridge with wife
Frances. Their visionary
partnership led to the
creation of the WEA

from trade unions and the Co-operative Societies, charitable donations and students' fees.

In these first years the organisation's growth was dramatic, irrespective of the criteria used. Mansbridge's youthful energy, his drive and commitment, allied to powerful individual and institutional support, maintained that momentum through to 1914. By then the WEA was accepted as part of the fabric of Edwardian social movements. Yet tensions within the organisation were emerging which would remain present throughout the 20th century.

By 1914 the WEA was already a complex organisation. There was a rich vein of organisational partnerships underpinning its development and public acceptance. There was now a proliferation of councils, committees, sub-committees and joint committees. Branches had been established, a District structure was in place with paid Secretaries, and thousands of students were attending hundreds of classes. All of this had been directed from two rooms "in a rather shabby office building in Buckingham Street, a turning off the Strand" with a staff which, in 1909, consisted of Mansbridge, two typists and occasional voluntary helpers.

It was inevitable that contentious issues would surface in the wake of the WEA's extraordinary momentum. Internal organisational arrangements

A commemorative plaque located in Windsor Road, Ilford, where Mansbridge was living in 1903

needed defining, especially the degree of autonomy which would be reserved for classes, Branches and Districts. The WEA's growth, and the possibility of a dramatic expansion of educational opportunities available to working class adults, also opened up discussion of what constituted appropriate provision for trade union students. Finally there was the question of manual workers' participation in WEA classes, and how Mansbridge's vision of intellectual and spiritual development would, or could, embrace education for economic and political emancipation.

These questions would continue to influence discussion and debate for much of the 20th century.

In June 1914 Mansbridge was diagnosed as suffering from cerebro-spinal meningitis. Remarkably he recovered – but progress was slow. Towards the end of 1915 he had been absent for more than a year and resigned as General Secretary of the WEA.

His successor was J M Mactavish, a one-time shipwright in the Portsmouth Royal Navy Dockyard, who served as General Secretary until 1928. He had made an impassioned speech on University tutorial classes for working class adults at the Oxford Conference in 1907. Under 'Jimmy' Mactavish the WEA's working relationships with the trade unions were to strengthen.

Although Mansbridge never again played a major role in the development of the WEA, he promoted adult education until his death in 1952. He remained active in the Co-operative movement and helped to found the World Association for Adult Education, the Seafarers' Educational Service and the British Institute of Adult Education, all of which survive today, in different forms, but nonetheless a continuing reminder of his organisational skills and campaigning zeal.

Above all, his abiding legacy is his vision of workers' education. His 1920 *An Adventure in Working Class Education* – the notion of 'adventure' as a description of his work being wonderfully apposite – talked of the "new opportunity" which lay ahead through social and economic change.

He wrote: "It may well be that the right use of sufficient leisure will enable men and women to realise once again their personalities by the exercise of their inborn gifts.

"Hitherto economic need and bad organisation have forced men away from the work they are fitted to do. In the future it may not be so. In the hours not spent in the mine or in the factory the workman will follow his own bent, read his books or even write them, exercise himself in music and song, and discover the secrets of life."

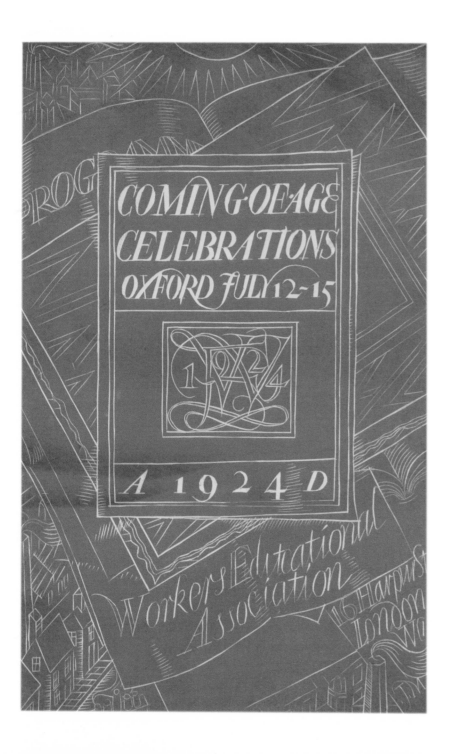

COMING·OF·AGE
CELEBRATIONS
OXFORD JULY 12-15

A 1924 D

Workers Educational
Association

16 Harpur St
London
WC1

Morning Session

Presidential Address—
Rt Rev. Lord Bishop of Manchester

Fraternal Greetings to the W.E.A.
will be conveyed from Trades Union
Congress General Council, Cooperative
Union, Working Men's Club & Institute
Union, National Union of Teachers,
Overseas W.E.A., Workers'
Educational Bureau of America,

Subject: "The Scope & Function
of Voluntary Associations in a
Public System of Adult Education"
Professor J.H. MUIRHEAD M.A. LL.D.

Afternoon Session

Subject: "The Place of the W.E.A. in the
Working Class Educational Movement"
Mr G.D.H. COLE M.A.

Two | Banded Together
Organisational Development

Since their inception in Reading in 1904, Branches have been the building blocks of the WEA. In line with Mansbridge's vision, it was expected they would be committed to the values of the organisation but would otherwise remain autonomous. Branches decided on the classes they wished to promote and made the necessary organisational arrangements.

The early Branches brought together the working class organisations the WEA aimed to serve, thus each Branch was very much a federal body. The few individual members in the first years were usually "highly educated men and women of University training". Alfred Zimmern, a lifelong Oxford supporter of the WEA, claimed in 1914 that the affiliated structure of the Branches was key to the "astonishingly rapid growth" of the WEA.

By 1905 there were eight Branches, which had risen to 219 by 1919. The numbers of affiliated organisations rose correspondingly from 100 in 1905 to 2526 by 1919. The first Scottish Branch was established in Springburn in 1905, and the first Welsh Branch formed at Barry in 1907. It was not until the inter-war period that any significant Branch development began in Northern Ireland.

The WEA adopted a Constitution to formalise the emerging structure in 1907, with powers devolved to Branches and Districts. At this time, only the North Western and Midland Districts existed, but by the outbreak of the First World War, new Districts had followed in South Wales, the North East, London, East Anglia, the South East, the West Country and Yorkshire.

Each District was governed by a Council representing affiliates, Branches and individual members, with national governance directed by

Growth of the WEA

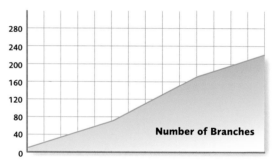

Number of Branches

Number of Affiliated Organisations

1905 to 1919

the Central Council with an elected Executive Committee. The assumption of autonomy built into the 1907 arrangements was taken further by the Constitutional changes of 1915, explicitly providing for the delegation of considerable powers to Districts. Further Constitutional change in 1930 – which placed, on paper at least, supreme authority with the National Delegate Conference – made little difference to the balance of power. In large measure this was the settled arrangement that remained in place until 1991.

Before the war in 1914 the WEA was an integral part of the working class 'movement', and in this way devolved responsibilities were understandable in practical and political terms. If the WEA could be described as a 'federal' body – as it was by some into the late 1980s – this was simply recognition of the nature of the organisational partnerships that gave the WEA credibility in the wider 'movement'. The WEA was built upon its partnerships.

Beyond the invaluable support of the Co-operative Societies and trade unions, many other organisations were attracted to the Association, from the Adult School Union to Working Men's Clubs. Political groups also affiliated in large numbers, and the 1911 WEA Annual Report recorded 64 Socialist or Labour clubs in affiliation.

THE EDUCATED WORKMAN.

Leading representatives of the University Extension movement were met on Saturday evening in Toynbee Hall by some 200 working-men delegates from forty London and provincial co-operative societies, ten trade unions, and similar associations. After a conference lasting an hour and a half, the meeting endorsed the action of the Oxford Conference in inaugurating an associated effort to develop the higher education of working men. It further, in view of the pressing need for systematised propaganda, urged working-class and educational organisations, and especially co-operative societies, to become affiliated to the association.

The Bishop of Stepney (chairman) and Mr. Churton Collins each sorrowfully showed how the high hopes they entertained some ten or fifteen years ago that University Extension lectures would be welcomed and patronised by the working classes had been doomed to disappointment.

Among the criticisms urged against the University Extension system as at present worked were that it was too "academic," and that more human interest was needed. The desire to learn more concerning the history of the co-operative movement, trade unionism, and kindred subjects should, it was thought, be more largely catered for.

At the 1903 Toynbee Hall Conference, over 150 delegates attended from 50 organisations. Reports of the Conference appeared in *The Daily Chronicle*, *The Labour Leader* (the newspaper of the ILP), and *The Times*, which gave 14 column inches to its report. *The Times* also covered the 1908 Delegate Conference in Birmingham, describing it as having the objective of "stimulating the development of education to suit the special needs of the working classes".

Left:
from *The Daily Chronicle*, 14 December 1903

The Executive Committee of the Rochdale Branch (Education Guild) in 1911. Of its 14 members, eight were described as working men, four as teachers, complemented by an ex-teacher and an employer

Given the WEA's interests, it was inevitable that activists were committed to many other working class organisations and activities. A survey conducted in Sheffield in 1918 highlighted a 27-year old engine tender, active in the National Union of General Workers and Co-operative movement, who attended WEA classes and University lectures on logic, theology and botany; an 18-year old munitions worker who participated in the Settlement House social study circle and WEA lectures, and a 24-year old machinist in a shell factory active in the Co-operative movement who enrolled in a WEA tutorial class on economics. From just a snapshot, a picture begins to emerge of the richness of working class activity and of the centrality of educational endeavour.

The WEA would always be more than a provider of education; its first National Delegate Conference, held at Toynbee Hall, Shoreditch in December 1903, demonstrated the shared commitment to social justice of the Association, Toynbee Hall and the University Settlements movement.

The Conference was presided over by the Bishop of Stepney, whose address highlighted the links between reform of elementary schools and

Rules and Programme
of Reading Branch in 1911.
Its committee membership
reflected the strong
relationship between the
WEA and working class
organisations affiliated at
local level

introduction of compulsory attendance at secondary schools, to securing working class access to Universities.

This was a reform package that the WEA would return to throughout its history. It was reiterated in 1917 when the WEA demanded post-war educational reform, lobbying for what was to become the 1918 Education Act, and also underpinned the 1942 campaign for a new post-war Education Act (introduced in 1944).

The WEA's early public advocacy of nursery education owed much to the influence of Margaret McMillan, who started pioneering open-air nursery schools for the under-fives in 1913-18. A former member of the Independent Labour Party (ILP), a powerful advocate of medical inspection and treatment of school children, she was a friend of Mansbridge and she actively supported the WEA from 1904. Mansbridge wrote: "With Margaret on our side there were few in the Labour Movement who doubted our integrity."

The WEA was unashamedly propagandist in its call for social change, and skilled at achieving public recognition of its views. Delegate

A zest for life and service to the WEA was demonstrated at all levels within the Association in the early years. There is no better example of this than T W Price (pictured). Born in Kidderminster in 1876, he moved to Rochdale in his teens where he became a warehouseman in a dyeing company.

Price joined the Social Democratic Federation, was attracted to Mansbridge's ideas, led two tutorial classes in Sociology and Economics that arose from dissatisfaction with Ruskin College correspondence courses, and became an executive member of the Rochdale Education Guild (as the WEA Branch in Rochdale was known) when it was founded in 1905. He was one of the 40 students in R H Tawney's pioneering Rochdale class on Economic History in 1908.

'T W' was clearly a remarkable individual; Mansbridge described him as a man whose "radiant personality never tired". In 1909 he was appointed District Secretary of the Midland District and played a major part in the establishment of the WEA Summer Schools, the first of which was held in Oxford in 1910.

When Mansbridge left for Australia in 1913, Price acted as General Secretary during his absence and subsequent illness. He took over Mansbridge's role as WEA Secretary to the Central Joint Advisory

Committee, an important mechanism for safeguarding the quality of tutorial class provision.

He co-authored, with Alfred Zimmern, *War and the Workers*, commissioned by the WEA's Executive Committee in 1915, which took the form of a study handbook on 'European history, international relations, and various economic, political and philosophical aspects of the war'.

This was followed in 1924 by his short history of the WEA, *The Story of the Workers' Educational Association, 1903-1924*, which carried an introduction by Tawney. In 1919 'T W' became Assistant General Secretary of the WEA. He died in 1945, just eight months after one of his sons was killed in action.

Munitions workers during the First World War. Throughout the war years the WEA continued to grow and to address the needs of an overwhelmingly manual working class constituency

A dinner party gathering at Balliol College in August 1909. The party included Mansbridge, T W Price, Zimmern, William Temple and A L Smith

conferences attracted huge support, as did public lectures on contemporary themes.

Eclectic in its partnerships, the WEA embraced an extraordinary range of activities. Nature rambles, art exhibitions, concert and theatre visits were common. Choirs and musical groups emerged. Branches published annual handbooks and publications proliferated at all levels. Book boxes and libraries were established, including a Central Library at Toynbee Hall in 1912.

But the extraordinary path of development seen up to 1919 started to falter. In 1924 future President G D H Cole spoke of the WEA as not knowing where it was going. Branches were becoming more the meeting place of individuals than gatherings of affiliated organisations. By then, 16 Districts were established, each serviced by a paid Secretary. From 1919 salaried tutors became part of the WEA landscape; the age of the unpaid tutor was ending.

Among the first tutor organisers to be appointed was Sophie Green. Her post was guaranteed initially by Mary Stocks (an influential supporter of the WEA nationally), and secured later by the Cassel Trust. A one-time tutorial class student working in a clothing factory, Sophie Green became tutor organiser in Kettering in 1919 and made working with women her priority.

In 1924 Districts in England and Wales attracted 'Responsible Body' status, and the direct receipt of Government grant created a greater

distance between Districts and the National Association. Districts participated in national life through the Central Council and National Conferences, but operated largely as autonomous bodies.

This left the 'centre' relatively weak and divided, and by 1927 relations between the General Secretary J M Mactavish and the Executive Committee were poor. Mactavish retired in 1928 and it was only with the appointment of Ernest Green in 1934 that any sense of effective leadership at national level re-emerged.

Yet there was no slowdown in the growth of educational activities. In 1924/25, 20,517 students participated in classes, rising to 29,879 by 1934/35. The main issue was the composition of the student body, especially how representative it was of the working class.

It was a critical question for an organisation distinguished from the start by its mission to serve the educational needs of the working class. This was the cement that held the Association together. If this was now contested, internally and externally, where was the WEA going?

Mactavish, R H Tawney and G D H Cole were among the keenest to maintain an undiluted focus on working class students, and in 1925 Cole declared:

"I want to serve the live-wired practical worker, who wants guidance in facing the practical problems of living."

The inter-war years, however, saw a steady decline of manual workers in the student body, as individual members took on a more dominant role in local and District affairs. Potentially much more contentious was the question of how far the growing dependency on Government financial support had encouraged the WEA, almost unwittingly, to weaken its links with working class organisations.

After the Second World War, the WEA emerged confident that it had made a valuable contribution during wartime and that reconstruction offered a dynamic future role. What it failed to appreciate were the accompanying social changes – a watershed had been reached and the traditional working class was changing.

In the early 1930s around a third of WEA students were manual workers, but by 1946 this had fallen to a quarter, and by 1956 was only one

TON IN FURNESS CO-OPERATIVE S
CADBURY'S
COCOA
PELAW POLISH
COLMANS
PELAW
BOOT POLISHES
BROMA
OPERATIVE
PURE
EXTRACT
COCOA

The Co-operative 'family' of organisations was a fertile recruiting ground for students to WEA classes into the 1950s. The weakening of student support in more recent times has been largely a reflection of social change

tenth. The WEA agonised over ways of reversing the trend or at least of coming to terms with it.

One path was to redefine its commitment to the needs of the 'working class'. In 1948 the notion of the 'educationally underprivileged' appeared, and by 1954 'serving a cross section of the adult population' was in vogue. In 1966 Constitutional change restated the WEA's aims as stimulating the demand of 'adults' for education, rather than 'workers' (although this was qualified with the words "in particular members of workers' movements").

Unless the Association introduced measures to direct the delivery of the course programme, it continued to run the risk of becoming a general provider of adult education. But intervention was never possible without undermining its very basis: the organisational autonomy of Branches and Districts.

From the early 1950s, a second and parallel route challenged Cole's 1952 assertion that the WEA could not have it both ways. Innovative and experimental projects were introduced, initially within the trade union education programme, then later in the 1960s and 1970s in community development and women's education. While this did not necessarily allow the WEA to be at ease with itself, it did provide evidence that it was coming to terms with the changing social landscape.

This was not the only long-standing issue the WEA struggled to resolve. In 1958 newly elected President Asa Briggs stressed the need to reinvigorate the WEA's voluntary movement, especially at Branch level.

By the early 1960s no more than 40% of WEA students were members. Membership had previously required an individual to sign up and 'opt in', thereby demonstrating the strength of the Branches. In 1966 this was fundamentally changed to define all students as members unless they specifically wished to 'opt out'. The immediate impact was to create a mass membership of over 100,000, but the real objective was to use the new arrangements to revitalise voluntary activism.

The 1966 Conference also agreed to a major re-examination of WEA policy, leading to the publication of *Unfinished Business* in 1969. This laid the basis for representations to the Government-appointed Committee of Enquiry into Adult Education, chaired by Sir Lionel Russell, whose recommendations confirmed what the WEA had hoped to hear.

There were four 'Russell priorities', as they quickly came to be known. Public legitimacy was offered in equal measure to the WEA's role in working in an industrial context; developing greater social and political awareness; creating opportunities for liberal and academic study below University level; and in providing opportunities for people experiencing social and cultural disadvantage. In these terms lay the compromise, apparently the answer to Cole's 1952 assertion, that yes, the WEA could be both general provider and provider to those most disadvantaged in society.

Throughout the 1970s there was dramatic growth in both trade union education and work with the 'disadvantaged'. Within the programme, new organisational forms were emerging at local level, in the form of WEA Trade

Newbattle Abbey, near Dalkeith, opened in 1937 as Scotland's first 'university of adult education'. The occupations of the college's students reflected its close relationship with trade unions, local authorities and the WEA. From 1950 Newbattle gave preference in its recruitment to students who had attended classes with the WEA, University extra mural departments, Settlements or local authorities

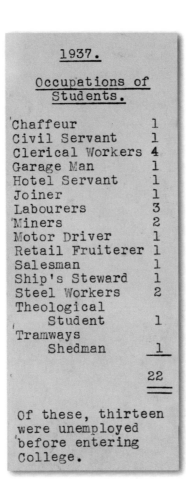

```
           1937.

         Occupations of
          Students.

Chaffeur              1
Civil Servant         1
Clerical Workers      4
Garage Man            1
Hotel Servant         1
Joiner                1
Labourers             3
Miners                2
Motor Driver          1
Retail Fruiterer      1
Salesman              1
Ship's Steward        1
Steel Workers         2
Theological
     Student          1
Tramways
     Shedman          1
                     ___
                      22
                     ===

Of these, thirteen
were unemployed
before entering
College.
```

Union Studies or Industrial Branches and Women's Studies Branches. By the end of the 1970s publications from these streams of work were enjoying an influence that extended far beyond the WEA.

The WEA had cause to celebrate its re-emergence as an innovative body working with unions and local communities, but the 'new work' had developed largely outside of 'traditional' Branch activity and was usually staff-led. Additionally, the 1966 membership change had not measurably increased voluntary activism, and the result was an emerging and unhealthy tension, compounded in the late 1980s by financial uncertainty and the dwindling of joint provision with Universities.

The Association's fortunes were turned around in the 1990s by externally-driven events. Following the merger of parts of the old Southern District with adjacent Districts, an Employment Appeal Tribunal judgement ruled that the WEA was a single employer. This, combined with the ending

WE TRAIN FOR ACTIVE

CITIZENSHIP.

Hand-illustrated records of the WEA in Lanarkshire for the 1945-50 period reflect the WEA's view of its role in wider society

of Responsible Body status, struck at the core of District autonomy and meant that the WEA was effectively a single organisation.

Constitutional change was inevitable, and the 1991 National Delegate Conference ratified proposals for what became known as 'integrated' Constitutional arrangements, on which the modern WEA has been built. Sadly, the North and South Wales and Northern Ireland Districts felt unable to participate in the new structures and withdrew from the National Association. In Scotland the three WEA Districts merged into a single Scottish Association, and the 'WEA England and Scotland' was born.

It was time to build commitment to, and confidence in, the National Association, which faced the immense task of merging disparate traditions, cultures and organisational arrangements. Yet unity could only grow with the recognition that diversity and local response should be celebrated as

organisational strengths, alongside the public authority that the new status of 'National Association' conveyed. This was greatly helped after 1992/93 by the WEA's transfer to the Further Education Funding Council (FEFC) for Government funding purposes.

The period to 2000 was one of financial growth, staff expansion and major development of the WEA's infrastructure, administrative and teaching facilities. The organisation was recognised as a powerful contributor to public policy debate, and by the end of the decade was referred to by the Chief Executive of the FEFC as "the star in the firmament" of adult education.

At its heart the WEA remained a membership organisation, the property of those who subscribe to its Charitable Purpose and Aims. By 2001 a new membership scheme was created, with the potential to revitalise active participation across the full breadth of the student body.

THE

WORKERS' EDUCATIONAL ASSOCIATION

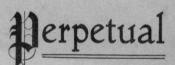

Perpetual

Calendar

This Calendar compiled by members and friends of the Kettering Branch in aid of District Funds

H. R., K.

The Workers Educational Association

PERPETUAL CALENDAR

JANUARY

1. **Dr. Albert Mansbridge (Founder of W.E.A.)**
"The spirit that urges the most gifted to keep in close and helpful touch with the lowliest is the spirit which is the source of all lovely and sublime expression."
Margaret McMillan

2. **Coun. H. J. Potter (Kettering)**
"We talk of independence,
There's no such thing on earth,
We live on one another
For all that life is worth."

3. "A passion for justice will accomplish nothing, without knowledge. You may become strong and clamorous, you may win a victory, but you will be trodden down under the feet of knowledge in the hands of privilege because knowledge will always win over ignorance."
Bishop Gore

4. **Coun. C. W. Clarke, Kettering.**
"Life is but a little holding, lent to do a mighty labour."

5. "By little strokes
Men fell great Oaks."

6. "Our nobleness of soul consists in steady love of what is good, steady scorn of what is evil."

7. **Mr. H. J. Thursfield, Kettering.**
"Take heed to that of God within you."

8. **Coun. Mrs. C. W. Clarke, Kettering.**
"Every new generation comes to us in tiny, helpless fragments of humanity, out of which a new world must be built of weal or woe."

9. **Miss Spencer, London.**
"O face of the true sun, now hidden by a disc of gold, may we know Thy Reality, and do our whole duty on our journey to Thy Light."

10. "Let men laugh when you sacrifice desire to duty if they will. You have time and eternity to rejoice in."
Theodore Parker

11. "It is one of the worst of errors to suppose that there is any other path of safety except duty."
Nevins

12. **Miss Margaret Smith, Kettering.**
"Life is a work, begin it,
Life is a battle, win it,
Life is a true heart, shield it,
Life is a sceptre, wield it."

13. "The proper way to check slander is to despise it; attempt to overtake it, and it will outrun you."
George Elliott

14. "God and one make a majority."
St. Teresa

15. "Sometimes the 'narrow way' lies through the crowd, and not away from it into the wilderness."
Thomas Lynch

16. "Learning without thought is labour lost, and thought without learning is perilous."
Confucius

17. **Mrs. G. Parker, Kettering.**
"We shall find happiness in love, in work and in beauty of all kinds; we shall find it in the expression of self, by means of a trained harmony, like that of a trained Orchestra, who become completely themselves in a common desire and a common satisfaction."
G. Crump

18. **Mr. F. Hill, Kettering.**
"He that striveth for the mastery is temperate in all things."
1 Cor. 9, 25

19. "God is faithful and he will not suffer you to be tempted above that ye are able, but will with the temptation also make a way of escape."
1 Cor. 10, 13

20. **Coun. S. C. Benford, Kettering.**
"The Moving Finger writes, and having writ
Moves on, nor all thy piety nor all thy wit
Shall lure it back to cancel half a line,
Nor all thy tears wash out a word of it."
Omar Kharyam

21. **F. E. Pearson, Northants. County Sec., L.N.U.**
"There is one thing stronger than all armies—it is an idea whose day has arrived."
Victor Hugo

22. **Mr. Harry Alford, Kettering.**
"Love in action is service—wrapped up in Goodwill delivered with Joy—and with no bill enclosed."
Margaret Cox

23. **Mr. J. Hawthorn, Kettering.**
"The spirit of delight, comes often on small wings."

24. **Mr. A. E. Buckby, Kettering.**
"Who steals my purse steals trash,
But he that filches from me my good name
Robs me of that which enriches him not
And makes me poor indeed.
Othello Act III, Scene III

25. **Mrs. Holland, Kettering.**
"Keep your smile in working order, you will need it before long."

26. **Mrs. Mann, Kettering.**
"Adversity is the trial of principle, without it man scarcely knows whether he is honest or not."

27. "Cast your bread upon the waters, though shalt find it after many days."

28. "It is the mind that lives; and the length of life ought to be measured by the number and importance of our ideas and not by the number of our days."
Wm. Cobbett

29. **Miss Roberts, Corby,**
"Divine love always has met and always will meet every human need."
Mary Baker Eddy

30. "Genius and ability are given as lamps to the world, not to self."
Sir Egerton Bridges

31. "Things done well, and with a care, exempt themselves from fear."
Shakespeare

Three | Co-operation not Incorporation
Relations with Government

Kettering Branch's Perpetual Calendar demonstrates the breadth and
depth of its members' interests. The calendar inevitably undated, is
thought to have been produced in the 1930s

Public recognition of the WEA, generated by the 1907 Oxford Conference and the 1908 Report, was formalised in the financial agreement reached with the Government's Board of Education. Besides any political motives it may have had, the Board was supportive of the WEA developing non-vocational adult education separately from the technical education beginning to be offered by Local Authorities. Universities would now meet half of the costs of tutorial classes, with the remainder paid for by the WEA out of grant support from the Board and Local Authorities. The so-called 'Golden Stream' of central Government funding was turned on, and the history of the WEA has been influenced by the organisation's relationship to the State ever since.

The Association soon and rather adroitly began to use grant support to fund one-year courses alongside the three-year tutorial classes, offering provision to students for whom tutorial classes were not necessarily appropriate. The Board supported this until 1917, when draft Regulations proposed switching all such funding to the Local Authorities, which would have given them exclusive responsibility for all non-vocational adult education outside of University tutorial classes.

However, this potential threat to the WEA's funding base was removed in 1919 with the publication of the Final Report of the Adult Education Committee of the Ministry of Reconstruction (chaired by A L Smith, Master of Balliol College). The Report recommended (in guarded language) that voluntary organisations including the WEA should receive direct grant support for one-year courses, and a commitment was given that there would be no grant changes for the next five years.

This period highlighted the potential vulnerability of the Association to shifts in public policy, and the issue that needed addressing was whether it could retain its independence if it ever reached a point where its survival

J M Mactavish was appointed General Secretary in 1915. His leadership saw the strengthening of relations with the trade unions and consolidation of the basis of state support

Oxford summer school students, 1912. A L Smith, later Master of Balliol, is standing on the right. Smith chaired the 1919 Adult Education Committee of the Ministry of Reconstruction

could be put at risk through the withdrawal of grant. If the WEA itself was unwilling to address this question, it would be constantly reminded to do so by the advocates of 'independent working class education' in the Plebs League, the Central Labour College (CLC) and the National Council of Labour Colleges (NCLC).

The WEA needed to proceed with great care. Pragmatically it was aware that state support was essential if healthy growth and development were to be maintained. At the same time there was a deeply held conviction that tutors and students were engaged in genuine enquiry, independent of faction, party or propaganda. There was risk attached, but the Constitutional arrangements in place led to the belief that the State would recognise the WEA's independence. It was prepared to submit to public scrutiny through inspection and reporting, but above all it believed in itself and its mission, and was satisfied that grant support could be arranged without undue controls or intrusiveness.

In 1924 the five-year moratorium on grant arrangements ended, and new Regulations were introduced whereby Government grant could be

The WEA was constantly challenged by advocates for 'independent working class education'. This book's cover illustration is taken from *Plebs* Magazine

paid to 'approved associations'. For the WEA this meant support for one-year and shorter course provision in non-vocational adult education, or liberal adult education in WEA terms. In addition WEA Districts in England and Wales became 'Responsible Bodies', able to receive grants and make provision in their own right. These arrangements were not extended to Scotland, where the WEA's Districts remained wholly dependent on the Local Authorities for public grant support.

For Mactavish and his colleagues this was a considerable achievement, considering that the War Cabinet had discussed the dangers of the WEA spreading Bolshevik ideas amongst the working class in 1917. The charge was considered serious enough for Mactavish to visit Buckingham Palace to assure the King there was no such intention. He was so persuasive that George V offered to become a subscriber! It is interesting to speculate what role William Temple may have played in this incident. President of the WEA from 1908, he had become Honorary Chaplain to the King in 1915.

The WEA was almost certainly saved from embarrassment during the War through its Constitutional block on 'outward' affiliation, which meant that it avoided being forced into a position of supporting either the anti-War Union of Democratic Control, or the pro-War Central Committee of Patriotic Associations.

King George V visiting Silverwood colliery. He offered to become a subscriber of the WEA following a meeting with J M Mactavish at Buckingham Palace in 1917. The meeting was prompted by concern from the War Cabinet that the WEA could spread Bolshevik ideas among the working class

By 1925 the President of the Board of Education, Lord Eustace Percy argued in his inimitable, exaggerated way: "£100,000 spent annually (on grants to the WEA) ...properly controlled, would be about the best police expenditure we could indulge in."

Further problems did arise in the 1920s, during the Second World War and during the Cold War, but there was never a serious threat to the integrity of the WEA or to the continuation of grant support. It was R A Butler who best described the guiding principle underpinning Government's relationship to organisations receiving grant support. In 1942, as President of the Board of Education he declared:

"The acceptance by a body of grant from the Board in respect of its educational work should not be taken as placing a limitation on the right of free speech enjoyed by its officers and members."

The 1924 grant aid framework remained in place until the early 1980s, with the only major challenge to its continuation coming in 1954. The then Ashby Committee of Enquiry, reviewing the organisation and finance of adult education, gave serious consideration to the dissolution of the WEA as an independent provider. The organisation was under growing pressure, firstly from the rapid expansion of Local Authority provision, and secondly from the prospect of

a dramatic weakening of the WEA's partnership with the Universities.

Although the Committee did not proceed with the recommendation, the text of the final Report provided little comfort to the WEA. A year later an article appeared in the *Times Educational Supplement* which challenged the WEA to be "an agent of democracy, bold, positive, engaged in the conflict of ideas" and, by implication, to reaffirm its founding values and become again a relevant social force.

Throughout the 1950s and 60s the financial base of the organisation was weak. The grant aid arrangements could meet the direct costs of

A play by the Bexley Branch
highlighted the often
contentious subject of
funding at all levels of
the Association

provision, but could not sustain sufficient growth in infrastructure to develop the WEA to meet the challenge of other providers in a rapidly changing society. Despite innovative work in trade union education and community provision, the WEA was treading water. Only in 1969, with the appointment of the Russell Committee of Enquiry into Adult Education, was confidence renewed in securing new funding that would address the WEA's development needs in part at least.

The Committee's Report, published in 1973, offered the WEA almost everything it had sought, legitimising in particular its developmental agenda. A similar process took place in Scotland where the Alexander Report recommended support for the Association's socially purposeful work. But it was 1976 before the Government responded with an additional £100,000 to sustain the development of what became known as the four 'Russell priorities'. Over the next six years real progress was made in meeting the mutually agreed targets, with further growth in trade union education high on the agenda.

But the momentum was broken by the election of the Conservative Government in 1979, which almost immediately withdrew the funding agreed by the Labour Government to support new staff appointments in trade union education. In 1983 the Department of Education and Science (DES) announced its intention to claw back grant from Districts' surpluses and to impose an 8.3% reduction in grant aid phased over the following three years.

The end of the 1980s were financially difficult for the WEA. Relations with the DES were conditioned by the recognition that there would be no fundamental improvement in grant support, and that consequently the WEA's interests might be best served through jointly reworking labyrinthine funding formulas.

As the Russell Report had strongly hinted, it was clear that the age of a 'contract' with the State based on 'general' grant support was over. The notion of a funding agreement emerged, which provided a given level of grant for the delivery of an agreed level of educational activities. By 1988 the DES had ceased to fund individual English Districts directly, instead making a single payment to the National Association which then determined the allocation between Districts.

In 1992 the Further and Higher Education Act provided for the independent incorporation of Further Education Colleges. Public funding would now be directed to the Colleges through the Further Education Funding Council (FEFC). The Government simultaneously decided to divest itself of major institutional funding responsibilities within the DES, including the provision of grant aid to the WEA. After 84 years, the direct funding relationship between Government ministry and the WEA was about to end.

Complex, lengthy negotiations and intensive parliamentary lobbying produced the agreement that the WEA's public funding would be routed through the FEFC. The WEA was given 'Designated Institution' status, bringing it within the scope of the 1992 Act for funding purposes.

Equally if not more significant, the Secretary of State formally advised the FEFC that grant payment to the WEA should be made to support not only 'Schedule 2' provision (courses which carried formal qualifications), but also non-Schedule 2 provision (courses which did not carry qualifications), which in 1992/93 represented some 70% of the WEA's educational programme.

At the heart of the FEFC funding arrangements was a simple two-way agreement – that, for a given sum of money, the WEA would deliver an agreed level of educational provision. Importantly this payment was made as a single block grant, leaving the WEA to determine the internal pattern and means of distribution.

In 1992/93 the FEFC grant represented some 60% of the WEA's total income (compared to typical College dependency of over 75%). The WEA's freedom to direct its most important income source in ways which best reflected internal needs was profoundly important to its well-being, with income from public funding increasing substantially as provision targets were exceeded. Money for growth was successfully secured, and the WEA reaped the advantages of a standard funding formula.

This was a period that saw the timeless WEA values of mutual support and respect back on the agenda, as the 1990s began to reflect major cultural and political shifts that allowed the guiding principles of the WEA to be seen as 'of the time'. The ideological fixation that denied the notion of 'society' and denigrated the value of 'collectivism' throughout the 1980s had been softened and replaced by a new emphasis on social responsibility, social cohesion, and the need to work towards a more 'inclusive' society.

The Labour election victory of 1997 saw the WEA's commitment to a more inclusive society in tune with public opinion and Government policy

The Learning and Skills Act 2000 saw the demise of the FEFC, and the creation of the Learning and Skills Council (LSC) in 2001 as the single conduit for central Government funding of post-16 education and training outside Universities. Immediately the WEA needed to agree the continuation of nationally-directed funding from the LSC – but in such a way that the Districts would still be able to access support from the LSC's local arms. The importance of this was underscored by the Government's decision to transfer grant support for Local Authority spending on adult community education to local LSCs.

Coupled with the potential decline in direct Local Authority support for its activities, the WEA was confronted with a much more competitive funding environment generally. Understandably, the LSC's early focus was on 16-19 year olds and on addressing 'skills gaps' in the labour market – presenting the WEA with a direct challenge to justify its role. Through the forceful reiteration of its social purpose, its commitment to addressing the needs of the most disadvantaged in society, and its continuing emphasis on achieving qualitative improvement in its educational activities, the WEA has maintained its position as a dynamic force in education.

© PA Photos

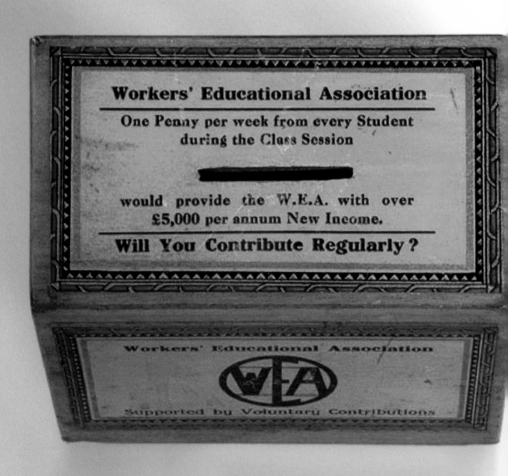

Workers' Educational Association

One Penny per week from every Student during the Class Session

would provide the W.E.A. with over £5,000 per annum New Income.

Will You Contribute Regularly?

Workers' Educational Association

W.E.A.

Supported by Voluntary Contributions

Four | Learning for Life
Students and Classes

This collecting box, dating from the 1950s, reflects the WEA's desire
to independently fundraise whenever and wherever possible

R H Tawney (seated centre, front row) and members of the Rochdale class in industrial history, March 1908. The first tutorial classes began in Rochdale and Longton in 1908, with R H Tawney as tutor. His 1914 reflections on his experiences as a tutor summed up all that was best in tutorial class provision: "Thanks to the fact that they are small, tutor and students can meet as friends, discover each other's idiosyncrasies, and break down that unintentional system of mutual deception which seems inseparable from any education which relies principally on the formal lecture. It is often before the classes begin and after they end, in discussions around a student's fire, or in a walk to and from his home, that the root of the matter is reached by both student and tutor."

Tawney was President of the WEA from 1928-44

The success of the WEA has always been judged by the quality and relevance of its educational activities. From the beginning the method of teaching, the purpose and practice of study, and the relationship between student and tutor needed to reflect the vision and values of the organisation. The choice of subject matter, it was assumed, would flow directly from interpreting how working class people could be spiritually and intellectually transformed. In this way the WEA would achieve a distinctive presence as both provider and advocate of working class adult education. Mansbridge captured the spirit of the WEA's approach:

"There was no test, implicit or otherwise, for admission, all that was asked being a willingness on the part of all to hear and to consider, with real respect, the arguments and facts brought forth to commend a case, even though it might appear to them (the students) to be wrong or defective".

The need to demonstrate formal educational attainment was rejected and replaced by a thirst for knowledge, a commitment to meeting the demands of organised study and a willingness to engage in the "full and free expression of the mind". Of great importance to the success of the early WEA was its recognition that, in this process of learning, the life and work experiences of working men and women formed a "vital principle" which would not be compromised.

The challenge for the early WEA was how to attract a critical mass of working class students into organised study. Mansbridge recognised that without the direct involvement of working class organisations, the 'adventure' could not succeed. Autonomous decision-making was encouraged from the outset, and alliances built with organisations at all levels which collectively represented the working class movement's commitment to the WEA as its educational arm. In this way the WEA could truly reflect, through its educational activities, the needs of working people.

Working class organisations were the transmission belt through which students would be recruited, resolving an otherwise impossible practical task. Such organisations enjoyed the support of working class men and women who had already taken the critical step of actively participating in collective endeavour. Irrespective of the club or society they belonged to, and often it was more than one, they had familiarity with the forms and expressions of coming together as a movement.

Some would have already participated in organised study, as was the case with Mansbridge himself. All had participated, through their involvement in club, Co-operative Society or trade union, in what we would today describe as 'informal' learning. Critically, many would have valued the opportunity for self-improvement that organised study offered them.

The essential building blocks of the WEA's distinctive contribution to adult education were coming together. Over time they would be formally expressed as a commitment to valuing life experiences; to validating the negotiated curriculum; and to the importance of sustaining external

ILFORD WOMEN'S CO-OPERATIVE GUILD. BRIGHTON OUTING. 24-6-2

partnerships alongside the internal partnership between student and tutor. It also embraced the relationship between individual and collective endeavour, and advocacy of socially purposeful educational activity. It was this dynamic, created through the combination of these approaches, which in a very real sense allowed the WEA to describe itself as a 'Movement' rather than an institutional provider.

Besides these partnerships, Mansbridge recognised the inestimable value of securing support from the Universities. They had entered the field in 1873 with the creation of the University Extension Movement, which had some success in appealing to working class audiences, especially in the North of England, but which, by the end of the 19th century, was attracting generally middle class supporters.

Extension provision usually took the form of a series of lectures, not necessarily on related themes. Fees were expensive, and audiences were of a size, often over 100, which restricted any possibility of effective student participation. Nonetheless, at the Oxford University Extension Summer School in 1899 Mansbridge raised the question of an alliance between University Extension and working class organisations, and it was in this context that the WEA was founded in 1903.

The initial aim of the WEA was to achieve its objectives by promoting much wider and deeper working class involvement in Extension provision. But by 1905 Mansbridge was concerned that the financial cost was becoming too large a burden, and that the lectures themselves did not offer

In the early years, women's participation in the WEA was marginal, reflecting society at the time. The gap prompted the formation of a Women's Advisory Committee in 1907 and the appointment of a Women's Officer in 1910

R H Tawney

the possibility of serious study and enquiry. It was out of this frustration, and continuing dialogue with Oxford, culminating in the 1907 Conference and 1908 Report, that the recommendation was made to jointly establish a network of tutorial classes to meet the needs of working class people, especially in the industrial towns and cities.

A Joint Committee with Oxford was established, and replicated with other Universities in England and Wales. In 1909 a Central Joint Advisory Committee was formed comprising the WEA, ten English Universities, the University of Wales and six University Colleges. Mansbridge was Secretary and William Temple was Treasurer, and its purpose was to promote and co-ordinate tutorial classes.

The first tutorial classes, organised on an experimental basis, began in Rochdale and Longton, North Staffordshire, in January 1908 with R H Tawney as tutor (Tawney was President of the WEA from 1928 until 1944). The model spread rapidly and by 1914 there were 14 Joint Committees in operation, sustaining 145 tutorial classes and attracting over 3,300 students. Social History and Economics were the pre-eminent subjects

Alfred Zimmern (left) wrote in 1914 that "unlike the middle class, the working class is habituated to corporate modes of life. The trade union, the club, the chapel, the co-operative society have kept alive for working people the instinct and habit of association".

Occupational analysis of students, 1928
from 378 students sampled in the West Midlands

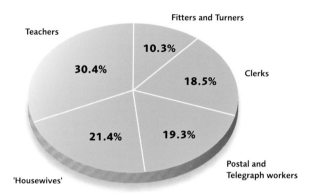

In 1928 a survey of West Midlands students vividly demonstrated changes in the student body since the pre-war years. The largest occupational group represented in the sample of 378 students was teachers (115), followed by 'housewives' (81), postal and telegraph workers (73), clerks (70) and, finally, fitters and turners (39)

(74 classes), followed by Modern History (22), Literature (17), Sociology (11), and Political Science (10). Just under half of the students were described as manual workers.

When Mansbridge and Temple undertook a study of the eight Oxford tutorial classes held in 1909, the student profile had shown a high concentration of manual workers, with a mixture of clerks, teachers and officers of various working class organisations. Men made up 91% of students, with over half the student body aged between 25 and 34, and 94% under 45.

The WEA was a 'Movement' in the making in the period to 1914, with the relative youth of its student body reflected in the age profile of its leading advocates, staff and officers. As the WEA matured as an organisation, its age profile would rise, a concern that led in 1936 to the appointment of Youth Officers.

It was addressing its defined constituency – those who were enjoined in other working class organisations and whose occupational base was in manual labour. In Edwardian Britain, society was such that the clerks who made up an important student group were not necessarily distanced from traditional working class culture.

The marginal nature of women's participation was a reflection of what society approved of as suitable at the time. In 1907 the huge gender gap led to the establishment of a Working Party on the Education of Women, the subsequent formation of a Women's Advisory Committee, and in 1910 to the appointment of a Women's Officer, Alice Wall. It was only with the extension of the franchise in the post-war period that there began a dramatic shift among women to seize the opportunities that education offered. By the 1930s, women were testifying to the liberating experience of attending tutorial classes.

The tutorial class was seen as the 'gold standard' by which all other forms of educational activity were judged. It was not the only form of provision however, and certainly not the largest, in terms of the total number of activities promoted or provided. Branches would promote single lectures and lecture series, study circles and discussion groups, as well as a host of informal activity. Activities would be

Bombs in the street.
The Second World War
posed a real challenge to
the WEA's work and
operational capacity, but its
vigorous response ensured
post-war growth

promoted in various forms, and of varying duration, for Co-operative Societies, trade unions and Adult Schools.

Tutorial classes were demanding of students. The commitment was to three years of study, to weekly class meetings of two hours per week over 24 weeks, and to systematic reading and fortnightly essay writing outside of the class. A maximum of 32 students could be enrolled in each class.

There was no questioning the clear sense of friendship and camaraderie that embraced students and tutors alike. Nor was there any doubting the high quality of much of their work. Students were rewarded on an individual level, in terms of recognition and self-fulfilment, and collectively as active participants in the transformation of the working class. They saw no contradiction between an individual's search for intellectual and spiritual enlightenment and helping to secure the social and material advance of working class communities.

What should not be forgotten is the level of personal sacrifice. Attendance at weekly classes and doing 'homework' was for many manual workers accompanied by long working hours, unpredictable overtime demands, the threat of unemployment, and the perennial search for private time and space to think and reflect. Unsatisfactory elementary education and lack of the formal skills of written communication were challenges many had to overcome.

Unsurprisingly students withdrew because of work or domestic pressures, or from a sense of not being able to cope with the demands of the class. The WEA organised 'reserve classes' to support aspiring students who might fill tutorial class vacancies.

Although the three-year tutorial class survived until the modern period, it was clear that, by 1924, manual working class participation was declining. The current trend was running toward shorter educational opportunities of one year or less. This was accelerated by an easing of Government grant arrangements for the funding of shorter courses, and new educational activities designed to meet the needs of trade unionists through the Workers' Education Trade Union Committee (WETUC).

By the late 1950s the proportion of manual workers participating in WEA provision had declined to one-tenth of total participants. The 'worker' was increasingly drawn from white collar, technical and supervisory grades, again reflecting social and employment changes. But the WEA's historic commitment to meet the needs of manual workers remained, and it berated itself for failing to address this constituency, at times almost consumed by self-doubt in a perennial search for the answer to the question, Where are the Workers? Tawney proclaimed that:

"Our business is not to organise classes for those whom, in the circumstances of today, it may, for one reason or another, be easiest to attract. It is to create a demand for education in individuals and bodies who at the moment may be unconscious of its importance to them but who, if a tolerable society is to be created, must be won to believe in it."

The answer would only come over time as the WEA began slowly to

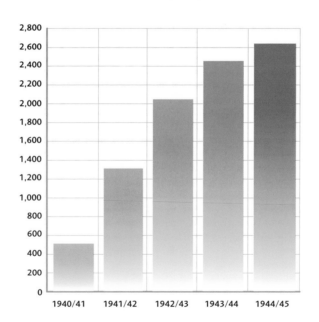

**London Branch Membership
1940-1945**

During the Second World War, the WEA's flexibility resulted in educational activities that truly met the needs of the time. These qualities attracted new activists in large numbers. In London, Branch membership rose from:
542 in 1940/41 to
1,333 (1941/42),
2,058 (1942/43),
2,447 (1943/44), reaching
2,619 in 1944/45.

This schedule of Branch classes shows how concern for post-war recovery dominated the programme in 1944-45

1944 -45.

POST WAR RECONSTRUCTION.

1. FOOD AND THE LAND   J. DUNCAN.
2. HEALTH.   DR. DUNLOP.
3. EDUCATION.   H.B. GUTHRIE.
4. HOUSING & TOWN PLANNING.   SAM BUNTON
5. INDUSTRY.   THOS. H. INNES.

LOCAL GOVERNMENT.   VARIOUS TUTORS.

EUROPE & OURSELVES.   LISTENING GROUP.

appreciate that the dynamic of social change required a pragmatic reinterpretation of its historic mission. This did not mean abandoning its vision and values, but it did demand a far greater responsiveness to external change and continual innovation. It also required the creation of new partnerships and the reinvigoration of traditional ones, and above all it had to recognise that its activities should be relevant to those students it wished to attract.

There is no better example of how extraordinarily responsive and imaginative the WEA could be than its work during the Second World War. In the first two years of war, Branch membership had fallen by a quarter and the number of tutorial classes by 40%. This was despite the Government's relaxation of the grant arrangements that lowered the threshold for funded courses from 12 students to eight.

Although all Districts responded well to the abnormal circumstances, wartime conditions in London posed a very special challenge. In the first year of war evacuation was already having an impact on organisational capacity; most of Ilford Branch's officers and committee members had been evacuated when war broke out, but nonetheless, the Branch had a 'good year'! Classes were arranged quickly at Guy's and Lambeth Hospitals, and across the District for refugees, particularly those who had escaped from Germany and Austria. A first course of lectures for the Army was provided, for an infantry training unit in South East Essex.

In 1941 the District began its programme of courses for Civil Defence

Post-war reconstruction was
underpinned by social
security legislation that
leaned heavily on Sir William
Beveridge's 1944 report

workers, with financial assistance from the WEA at National level. By 1945, 187 courses had taken place, due largely to the extraordinary efforts of the part-time organiser, Ms C H Oppenheim. The success of the programme in London resulted in its expansion across the WEA, again with grant support from the Association nationally for the appointment of part-time organisers.

The arrival of American forces in London and the South East by 1942 was used creatively to launch a programme of lectures, 'What is America?' delivered by US personnel. The District simultaneously promoted classes on 'Post-War Reconstruction', followed by public meetings, conferences and one-day schools on 'Education' aimed at informing public opinion and urging Government to introduce a new Education Bill into Parliament. By 1944, the District's classes on 'International Relations' and post-war 'Problems' were as popular as its 1930s staples of Psychology, Literature and Music.

Late in the war, the Leyton Branch, with the support of the Education Committee of the local council and Essex County Council, opened an Adult Education Centre where the WEA was introduced to the community through music recitals and socials. Within months the premises were described as too small, and more spacious accommodation was sought.

The Ministry of Information sought the help of London Branches in arranging film shows. Guildford Branch arranged 'gramophone concerts' in co-operation with NALGO, the local government trade union, while the Surbiton Branch raised £90 through a bring-and-buy sale for the

ZERO HOUR FOR THE CURATE

Clement Attlee celebrating
the Labour Party's election
victory in 1945

A Nottingham 'housewives'
class. The WEA long believed
that those who described
themselves as 'housewives'
were largely from working
class communities, but no
contemporary evidence
was ever produced. By 1959
it had become clear that
married women in WEA
classes generally tended
to come from "higher
social categories"

Red Cross Prisoners of War Fund. Not to be outdone, Westminster and West London Branches organised a highly successful dance "within the shadow of the Houses of Parliament".

By 1945 the number of Civil Defence workers classes began to decline, and the District turned its attention to the needs of building trades workers brought to London to repair bomb-damaged homes. Some 10 courses lasting between six and 12 meetings were organised. Similar provision was made in Surrey and Middlesex in Women's Land Army hostels.

The war experience presented the Association with a challenge: could it take forward these inestimable gains? Could it build a new generation of support in a very different Britain? Could it use the high profile it had achieved through campaigning around reconstruction to influence policy-makers at national and local levels?

Theoretically the election of a Labour Government in 1945 could only be advantageous. Fourteen Ministers in the new Government, including the Prime Minister and the Chancellor of the Exchequer, and over 50 MPs were closely linked to the WEA as former students, tutors or as members of its Executive Committee. Alfred Zimmern proclaimed with forgivable exaggeration that:

"It is an England moulded by the WEA that has been swept into power".

This was just the tip of the iceberg. The WEA's impact on the lives of its students and tutors since its very beginning was a powerful force through which it could build its future. There was eloquent testimony from many individuals and locations.

A Learning French
'experimental' class at
Olympia in the 1950s,
taught by Elizabeth
Monkhouse, who was
later to become Deputy
President of the WEA

Near Left: Natural History class at Frensham Ponds, Surrey

Left: Architectural students on a 'field trip' in the 1970s

Where students wrote or spoke of their experiences with the WEA they often highlighted recurring themes: they believed their power of impartial analysis had increased, they felt a sense of intellectual enfranchisement or an end to intellectual isolation. They reflected on their ability to see the world as a whole, of how individual life fitted into wider society. For many manual workers there was a strong sense that they had escaped from the 'industrial machine'.

These individual benefits were invariably linked to a keen sense of social purpose. Students reflected on the value of social interaction and recognised how they could 'give back' to where they came from. For some this meant new or renewed commitment to working class organisations. Others went on to become tutors with the WEA. It was this mix of individual enrichment and concern for social justice that emerged again and again. Students' enquiring spirits matched the WEA's vision and values, and each fed off the other for mutual benefit.

The tragedy for the WEA in the post-war period was that rekindled working class enthusiasm for education soon faded. These were times of profound changes in social attitudes and expectations. Nothing was forever – least of all the 'truths' and loyalties of the pre-war generations.

In 1953 the WEA published a Report, *Adult Education: Why this Apathy?* by the then General Secretary Ernest Green. He looked in detail at the town of Stockport in 1949/50, surveying a wide range of attitudes, and found that one adult in 46 was participating in an Evening Institute class, while only one in 265 was taking a class in the Liberal Arts. Of his sample of 414 parents, 81% wanted a greater emphasis on vocational training in schools; 56% regretted the raising of the school-leaving age to 15 in 1947; and 84% were opposed to it being raised to 16.

Other surveys proved equally depressing. A 1962 Gallup Poll in North Staffordshire found that 83% of working class respondents had never heard of the WEA. A 1965/66 survey in Chester and Eccles found that only 1% of semi-skilled and unskilled workers had ever taken a WEA or University Extra Mural course.

When Thomas Kelly, Director of Extra Mural Studies at Liverpool University, wrote to the *Guardian* in March 1953, he applauded the proportionate expansion in short course provision (referred to as 'elementary' provision at the time). His argument was simple:

"It seems clear to me that if the WEA is to reach, as it is constantly being urged to reach, an ever-widening circle of working-class students

Neil Kinnock, former Labour Party Leader and now European Community Commissioner, was formerly a WEA tutor organiser in South Wales from 1966-1970

it must provide a much greater range and variety of elementary courses."

Paradoxically, in 1953 the WEA was providing more tutorial classes than ever before – with a disproportionate rise in short course provision and a sharp decline in manual working class participation.

The WEA was changed fundamentally. Gone was the presumption of a mission which would draw the working class like a clarion call. From the late 1950s on, the Association was challenged in its mission. New constituencies were defined as provision became more tailored to specific groups in the community.

There was much experimental work, firstly in provision for trade unionists, later extended into educational activities designed for the needs of working class communities. By the 1970s innovative work was emerging in women's education and with Black and Asian communities. The commitment to tutorial and sessional classes continued, although as time passed Branches tended to drive down the length of individual courses.

This 'new' work was largely organised outside of Branch provision, which continued to be the dominant feature of WEA life. Not until the 1990s did the map of WEA provision begin to change significantly. By this time opportunities had opened up with myriad locally-based community groups as well as statutory bodies and agencies. In 1999, research commissioned by the WEA suggested that at District and local levels there were some 1,600 formal partnerships across the Association underpinning the educational programme.

The dramatic expansion of Community Learning provision from the mid-1990s to 2001 (from 30% to 42% of total activity) owed much to the creative exploitation of partnership opportunities at local level. It was this work that tied in perfectly with the public policy commitment to 'social inclusion' and community 'capacity building'. For the WEA it was affirmation of its own historic commitment to meet the learning needs of those most disadvantaged in society.

These developments took place within the context of substantial expansion in the educational programme as a whole. From 1995 to 2001, growth was at times dramatic; between 1995 and 1999, student enrolments increased by 25%. What was even more significant for the WEA's future development was the recognition that each of the three streams of activity – Community Learning, Workplace Learning and the publicly advertised, locally promoted General programme – were equally valued as vital components of its work.

GENTLEMEN

Five | Labour and Learning
The WEA and trade unions

Saturday Night at the Club by Oliver Kilbourn (1940). The Ashington
Group of miner artists grew out of WEA courses in art in this
Northumberland mining community in the 1930s

The appointment of 'Jimmy' Mactavish as General Secretary in 1915, according to Mary Stocks, owed much to the view that as "Mansbridge had tipped the balance of the Association on the side of the universities, it was now time to tip it on the side of the trade unions". The WEA had always anticipated support from trade unions; students were drawn from them, while some union leaders were prominent advocates of an alliance between organised labour and the WEA.

At the 1908 meeting of the Oxford/WEA Joint Committee, individual unions and the Parliamentary Committee of the Trades Union Congress (TUC) were represented through the WEA's Advisory Committee. Important initiatives were also happening locally, with trades councils organising meetings leading to new WEA Branches in Leicester, Northampton, Derby, Blackpool and Glasgow. A WEA presence in Belfast owed much to a joint trades council and Co-operative movement initiative; the WEA's first Branch at Reading had a trades council representative on its Committee from its foundation in 1904. There was reciprocation here as well: the WEA Branch in Ilford helped to set up the local trades council.

In 1911, the WEA Annual Report revealed that 150 individual trade union branches and trades councils were affiliated to seven of the WEA's largest Branches – Birmingham, Blackburn, Bristol, Leeds, Reading, Rochdale and Sheffield. Although relationships with unions were warm, neither side was especially proactive in developing them before 1915.

In 1909 students at Ruskin College went on strike, leading to the establishment of the Central Labour College (CLC) the same year. Progressively this became a direct challenge to any claim the WEA

Arthur Pugh, General Secretary of the Iron and Steel Trades Confederation. Mactavish's discussions with Pugh led to the creation of WETUC in 1919

might make to be the educational wing of the Labour Movement. From operating Extension classes in Rochdale in 1909/10, the CLC was by 1914/15 operating in 18 centres across the UK. Its student support came exclusively from trade unions, primarily from the Amalgamated Society of Railway Servants (later the National Union of Railwaymen) and the South Wales Miners' Federation.

The CLC's early invective for the WEA was summed up in the first issue of its *Plebs* magazine in 1909 (the WEA journal *The Highway* had first appeared in October 1908):

"The number of attempts to impose education from 'above' are legion. Prominent among them stands the University Extension movement with its powerful ally the Workers' Educational Association... Workers who have thought their way to an independent movement will recognise a parallel between these movements in the field of education and the Radical and Lib-Lab movements in the field of politics."

The CLC believed the WEA had hopelessly compromised itself through its alliance with the Universities and its acceptance of funding from the State. The CLC, and from 1921 the National Council of Labour Colleges (NCLC), would offer 'independent working class education' paid for, and controlled by, "the definite class organisations of the workers". Its approach to education was founded on a narrow and mechanistic treatment of Marxism and open to the criticism that it was little more than propaganda.

In 1915 the CLC challenge was real enough for Mactavish to immediately strengthen the WEA's relationships with trade unions. His 1916 pamphlet *What Labour Wants from Education* provided a vital reference point for a new organisational partnership. Critical to this were his discussions with Arthur Pugh, General Secretary of the Iron and Steel Trades Confederation (ISTC). A framework emerged, from a scheme initially designed to meet the educational needs of ISTC members, which led to the creation of the Workers' Education Trade Union Committee (WETUC) in 1919.

Individual unions committed financial support that directly reflected the demands they made for educational activities organised by WETUC, and the WEA provided administrative and teaching support. By the early 1920s full-time tutor organisers were appointed by the WEA to service WETUC provision, which soon took the form of tutorial classes, weekend and summer schools, Branch lectures, and the availability of a lending library. Importantly, WETUC activities were partly financed through the WEA's public grant support.

CAST ADRIFT

By a large majority the A.G.M. decided to withdraw from Ruskin College and support the Central Labour College

From the Railway Review 29-x-1909

The scheme was controlled by the WETUC Education Committee, a joint committee of the WEA and affiliated trade unions with the latter in the majority. Pugh was Chairman, Arthur Greenwood (Chairman of the WEA Yorkshire District and later Secretary of the Labour Party's Research Department) was Vice-Chairman, and Mactavish was Secretary. G D H Cole (a tutor in the London University Extra-Mural Department, and later WEA President) also exercised tremendous influence on WETUC's development.

WETUC quickly secured the support of other unions, including the TGWU and National Union of General and Municipal Workers, until 27 were in membership by 1939. That year the scheme supported 191 three-year tutorial, one-year sessional and single term classes, and 86 day and weekend schools. WETUC was to remain the backbone of the WEA's provision for trade unions until 1963.

WETUC and CLC/NCLC were competing for the same students, and this fuelled their ideological animosity and the extraordinary sharpness of much of their public debate. But there is evidence to suggest another reality emerged when it came to students deciding which course they wished to attend. One student in 1925 spoke for many when he declared:

"The average worker-student does not care twopence about the WEA and NCLC squabble. With most workers it is a matter of chance in which movement they eventually find themselves. They join a class in the first place because the time, place, or subject, is convenient to them, or because

The General Strike, 1926, by Cliff Rowe, a working class artist and founder of the Artists International Association. The painting was one of five commissioned by Walter Stevens, General Secretary of the Electrical Trades Union in the 1950s, a union which was never to affiliate to WETUC

a fellow worker has persuaded them to join that particular class, the principles on which the class is organised are very seldom considered."

From 1926, with the defeat of the General Strike and the relative retreat of organised labour until 1939, the ideological differences between the WEA and NCLC were articulated with less venom. The NCLC had to moderate its position to retain financial support from its trade union affiliates, and in return became increasingly vulnerable to criticism from the Communist Party.

The TUC attempted to address the rivalry in 1925 with a proposal to bring together the NCLC, the CLC, the WEA and Ruskin College within a TUC Education scheme (known as the Easton Lodge proposal). Despite two years of discussions attempting to create unity in the delivery of trade union education, it came to nothing. The potential partners failed to

G D H Cole, tutor in the London University Extra-Mural department and WEA President. Cole played a major role in the development of WETUC

surmount their differences, in part fuelled by serious internal disagreements in both organisations. The loser in the short-term was the CLC which closed in 1929, unable to survive financially.

In the inter-war period, WETUC's fortunes closely followed the economic cycle and its impact on trade union organisational strength. After 1926 WETUC activities dipped sharply, only beginning to recover in the early 1930s. Its administration was rejuvenated by the appointment of Ernest Green as WEA Assistant General Secretary in 1929. Responsible for creating a more unified programme of provision, Green supervised the introduction of WETUC correspondence courses and published the series of short textbooks known as the Sixpenny Library which ran from 1934 to 1939. In the eight years to 1939 a further 16 trade unions affiliated to WETUC, bringing the total to 27.

WETUC continued to be active during the war years. Understandably there was relative decline in the provision of weekend schools but this was compensated for by a dramatic increase in the delivery of day schools. By 1955, 385 classes were provided with well over 12,000 students attending day and weekend schools.

But evidence was emerging to suggest the beginnings of a dramatic transformation in educational provision for trade unionists. Outside of the correspondence courses, WETUC activities were very much concentrated in subject matter which assumed the students' primary interests were in understanding the history, culture and condition of the working class. Economics, politics and history, as well as literature and music, constituted the core of the curriculum – not dissimilar from the WEA Branch programme. Herein lay the problem. During the post-war period trade

THE WORKERS' EDUCATIONAL ASSOCIATION

SPECIAL CONFERENCE

of

Representatives of Affiliated Trade Unions

to discuss

Education to Meet the Modern Needs of Trade Unions

BONNINGTON HOTEL, SOUTHAMPTON ROW, LONDON, W.C. 1.
WEDNESDAY, 11th MAY, 1949.

Sessions : 11.0 a.m. to 1.0 p.m.
2.30 p.m. to 4.30 p.m.

The Conference will be opened at 11.0 a.m. by
MR. HAROLD CLAY,
President, Workers' Educational Association.

An Introductory address will be given by
PROFESSOR R. H. TAWNEY,
Vice-President, Workers' Educational Association.

The Conference will adjourn for lunch at 1.0 p.m. and resume at 2.30 p.m.

unions, and especially the TUC, were beginning to identify new priorities in education which reflected the day-to-day needs of union lay office-holders.

In 1949 the WEA convened a special conference in London on the theme of 'Education to Meet the Modern Needs of Trade Unions'. WEA representatives included Harold Clay and R H Tawney (WEA President and Vice-President), and General Secretary Ernest Green. The most significant contribution came from Alan Winterbottom, the TUC's Director of Studies from 1946, whose concerns were how training could help to create a cadre of 'competent representatives', and how the roles of unions and the TUC in the provision of training should be defined. He challenged the WEA to come up with proposals that would allow it to 'assist' in this process.

The WEA responded in 1954 with three Pilot Area schemes in trade union education in Cleveland, Port Talbot and Tyneside. Evaluation of the Pilot, and a general survey of educational opportunities for trade unionists, was presented to the 1959 WEA National Conference. It argued that there was not necessarily a contradiction between 'education' and 'training', thus

Right: Steel industry students take advantage of WEA day release training in 1970. The popular chart teaching method also features in an outdoor session at a WEA residential school for trade unionists (below)

validating both a Workers' Education tradition ('education') and post-war trade union education ('training'). The questions the report posed were whether the two 'traditions' could co-exist within the WEA, and what, if any, was the future role of WETUC.

The development of paid day release for lay office-holders during the early 1950s, and rapidly from 1958, focused the unions' attention on what constituted an appropriate curriculum and how it would be delivered. There was consensus that it should concentrate on the practical tasks faced by shop stewards and other lay representatives, but how would consistency be achieved and what institutional arrangements would support delivery?

These questions prompted the TUC again to attempt to consolidate education provision for trade unionists. A report to the 1959 TUC Congress recommended the integration within its own Education Department of Ruskin College's correspondence courses and the combined operations of WETUC and the NCLC. While the WEA soon

An early attempt to give women a stronger voice in their unions. A WEA course for women members of the TGWU, Cirencester in 1959

The Women Against Pit Closures pressure group maintaining a vigil outside Armthorp Colliery in Yorkshire, 1984. The 1980s miners' strike was a turning point for the union and for many women in mining communities

© John Harris/reportdigital.co.uk

accepted the absorption of WETUC into the TUC, there were protracted negotiations with the NCLC on its integration. In 1963 a final scheme was agreed which marked the end of WETUC. The WEA's provision aimed at the needs of trade unionists would now be delivered predominantly through the TUC Regional Education Service.

The dramatic expansion of the TUC's regional programme was prompted by the 1968 publication of its major strategy document, *Training Shop Stewards*. Initially the programme was funded directly through affiliation fees, but the development of the 'Social Contract' and new employment legislation in the mid-1970s led to grant support from the Government to the TUC in 1976.

With the focus directed almost exclusively at union representatives and a regional framework for delivery in place, the period to 1979 was one of dramatic expansion. In 1979 over 34,000 students participated in the TUC regional programme, of which over 20% were students on courses delivered by the WEA through the TUC scheme.

Shortly before its fall in 1979, the Labour Government had agreed to fund a raft of full-time trade union studies appointments across the Association. This would have consolidated the WEA's position as a major provider of union education, but it was slow to seize the opportunity due to disagreement amongst Districts, and the incoming Conservative Government withdrew the offer. This indecision had a negative impact on the TUC's attitude to its future relations with the WEA.

Throughout the 1970s and 80s, the WEA's programme for trade unionists was dominated by workplace representative training under the TUC scheme. During the 1980s however the TUC began to consolidate its

The 'Social Contract' and new employment legislation led to government grant support for WEA/TUC trade union provision in the 1970s. Pictured on a TGWU Conference platform are some of the main architects of the Social Contract

(left to right): Len Murray, TUC General Secretary, James Callaghan, Prime Minister, Stan Pemberton, TGWU President, Jack Jones, TGWU General Secretary, and his wife Evelyn, and Moss Evans, Deputy TGWU General Secretary

The WEA's partnership with Unison in the Return to Learn programme delivered new opportunities for the most vulnerable and least formally qualified in the workplace. The quality of its programme laid the groundwork for further union and public sector partnerships

regional programme within Colleges of Further Education and through regional centres, to the point where WEA provision was becoming confined to a limited number of Districts.

Despite the weakening of the TUC programme, commitment to long-standing partnerships with trade unions remained strong and in 1989 the WEA began to develop a new form of provision that would shift the emphasis of its offer to trade unionists and re-ignite programme activity across the whole of the WEA.

Initially working with the National Union of Public Employees (NUPE) and then UNISON, the WEA began to address the needs of the most vulnerable and least educationally qualified in the workplace. Thus began the 'Return to Learn' programme, subject to a National Partnership Agreement between UNISON and the WEA in 1995, and which by 2000 was delivered throughout the Association.

Public acclaim for the quality of the work opened up further major opportunities within the public sector, with the National Health Service Executive and the University for Industry (UfI Learn Direct). Through such partnerships, the WEA's historic mission to meet the educational needs of workers and trade unions was reflected in a vibrant and contemporary setting.

Dinner ladies receive certificates on completing the UNISON/WEA Return to Learn programme

THE HIGHWAY

PRICE 2ᴰ   PRICE 2ᴰ

Six | A Transferable Idea?
International Partnerships

At the WEA's Constitutional Review Conference in 2000, a unanimously agreed change was made to its operating Principles. For the first time in WEA history, its Constitution explicitly declared a commitment to internationalism in its work. Here was recognition of the importance of current international activities and their guiding values, and of the WEA's tradition of embracing international responsibilities to a Workers' Education movement that transcended national boundaries.

From its earliest days the WEA's work attracted interest beyond Britain. A French research student from Paris produced a doctoral thesis on the WEA in 1910, and Mansbridge indicated that visitors had travelled from Germany, Denmark, Chile, Japan, the United States and Belgium "to marvel at the spirit of the movement". A WEA-type tutorial class was formed in Cologne about that time but failed because of hostility from the University and the German Social Democratic Party. Certainly in the period before the First World War, the WEA's Oxford and Cambridge Summer School meetings attracted regular visitors from the Dominions.

The enthusiastic reaction of colleagues from abroad convinced Mansbridge of the possibility of the WEA model being transplanted elsewhere. His target was Australia, not least because William Temple had lectured on the tutorial class system during his visit to Adelaide in 1912, and where the Sydney Trades and Labour Council was considering the establishment of a WEA. Mansbridge left for Australia in June 1913, returning in January 1914. Two months after his return a WEA was established there.

This early venture, although successful, was somewhat exclusive in its intent. The objective of transposing, root and branch, the WEA's approach to workers' education did not fully recognise the specific conditions that had allowed it to develop in Edwardian Britain. Where there were arguably major political, social and cultural ties that could draw in the Dominions, this was not the case elsewhere, especially in Europe and the United States, where very different forms of workers' education were being established.

In 1919 the Australian WEA asked the WEA's Executive Committee to consider forming some kind of international association. The WEA offered to develop a scheme "linking up ourselves with *similar organisations* throughout the world" (italics added). A policy statement setting the context was prepared by Arthur Greenwood, a member of the Executive Committee, and published as a *Memorandum on the WEA and its Foreign*

The concept and ideals of the early WEA transferred most readily to the Empire. At his Coronation Durbar in Dehli in 1911, King George V announced his decision to transfer the seat of the Imperial government from Britain to Dehli

Arthur Greenwood, Chairman of the WEA Yorkshire District, was a major influence on the international policy of the WEA. In an illustrious parliamentary career he was Minister of Health in the 1929 MacDonald Government, Minister without Portfolio in the Churchill War Cabinet, and respectively Lord Privy Seal, Paymaster General and Minister without Portfolio in the 1945 Atlee Government. Greenwood was opposed to the Labour Party's entry into MacDonald's National Government in 1931 and became an outspoken critic of appeasement in the late 1930s. In 1935 he was elected deputy Leader of the Labour Party and from 1942 to 1945 was acting Leader of the Labour Party in the House of Commons

Policy. This was the only major statement on international co-operation produced by the WEA in the inter-war period. It was accepted in principle, together with the proposal to convene:

"A Conference of WEA representatives *from all parts of the British Commonwealth*, to which representatives from workers' educational movements in other countries may be invited" (italics added).

But in 1920, probably due to staff being committed to other work, it was decided not to go ahead with the Conference. Despite this, Workers' Educational Associations continued to develop in the Dominions. By 1923 they had been formed in Canada, New Zealand, South Africa and Tasmania (as well as 'mainland' Australia). There is also evidence that a WEA had been formed in Madras in 1920.

But what of co-operation beyond the Empire? The WEA Executive Committee could hardly have failed to notice the landscape on the left of European and US politics was changing dramatically, which in turn would influence any international collaboration. The domestic schism with the CLC/NCLC exemplified the potential problems faced by a non-party political organisation like the WEA. Take for example the differences between the WEA and ABF, the Swedish Workers' Education organisation,

Delegates to the 1924 IFTU conference in Oxford. David Ben-Gurion is standing in the back row (sixth from the right)

The first WEA/ILO summer school was held in Geneva in 1934

formed in 1912 and much influenced by the Danish Folk High School Movement. In the early 1920s ABF affiliated with, at national level, the Social Democratic Party and its Youth wing and the Communist Party and its Youth organisation.

Contact was maintained with other organisations but outcomes were rarely positive. The WEA attended the International Conference on Labour Education in Brussels in 1922, but little resulted. Nevertheless, a follow-up Conference convened by the International Federation of Trade Unions (IFTU) was held at Ruskin College two years later, almost certainly with support from the WEA. A total of 59 delegates from 20 countries attended, with Mactavish representing the WEA. He came under bitter attack from the NCLC General Secretary but maintained tremendous dignity throughout. Unquestionably the IFTU had brought together a quite extraordinary gathering of 'left' trade union leaders from Europe, Asia and the Americas – among them David Ben-Gurion, identified as the representative from 'Palestine'.

The conference agreed to establish an International Federation of Labour Organisations concerned with Workers' Education, but sadly the venture stalled and, for the WEA, marked the end of contributing to the development of an international body of workers' education organisations until 1943.

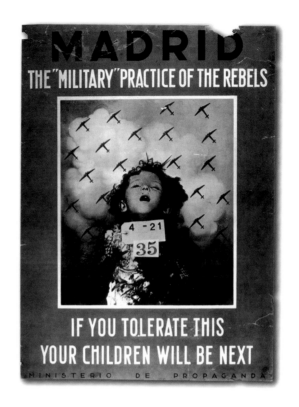

The Spanish Civil War in the
1930s was a terrible taste of
things to come. It generated
deep conflict in the WEA.
The Highway's publication of
pro-Franco articles by Arthur
Bryant, under the editorship
of W E Williams, led to the
intervention of the WEA's
Central Executive Committee
and to subsequent reviews
of content

The appropriateness of co-operating with organisations whose form and direction contrasted with that of the WEA was never resolved in the inter-war period. The Association took the route of least resistance, primarily supporting those bodies constructed on the WEA model, almost exclusively found in the Dominions. With the international crises of the 1930s, the WEA found it difficult to position itself at an organisational level. It was left to the individual – as a tutor, student, staff or committee member – to engage in personal or group activity beyond the WEA, perhaps stimulated by WEA classes.

The WEA's first contact with inter-governmental bodies came in 1934, when an international summer school was held in Geneva in co-operation with the International Labour Office (ILO), then an agency of the League of Nations. Organised by WETUC, 40 students attended, all trade unionists. It continued annually as a two-week event until 1938. It is intriguing to speculate the extent of Alfred Zimmern's role in its development – a powerful influence on the League of Nations' Council, Assembly and Secretariat, from 1925-39 he was also Director of the School of International Studies in Geneva.

The school may also have been inspired by the early work of Mary Macarthur, Secretary of the National Federation of Women Workers and one of the founders of the National Anti-Sweating League in 1906, a vocal

RUSSIA WAS OUR ALLY.

CHOSSUDOWSKI
ON
PROBLEMS OF MODERN RUSSIA.

Post war readjustments.
A drawing advertising a
course documents how the
Cold War had impacted on
international relations

supporter of the ILP and Britain's 'worker representative' to the founding conference of the ILO in Washington in 1920. She was known to J J Mallon, National Treasurer of the WEA, she was committed to securing educational opportunity for working women, and she bequeathed trust funds which until the 1990s helped to sustain women's participation in the annual WEA/ILO Study Project.

From 1939 the WEA's war experience at home and overseas helped to shape the future direction of its international work. The Association was committed to meeting the increased wartime demand for organised learning. There was concern initially within the Board of Education that the WEA's advocacy of free discussion in classes on 'controversial' subjects would provoke protest and raise potential national security questions, especially in provision for members of the Armed Forces.

In 1942 the Army Council introduced a programme known as The British Way and Purpose, or BWP. It was delivered through members of the Army Education Corps and by civilians secured by the Central Advisory Council for Adult Education in HM Forces. WEA tutors were recruited through each route. So much of the programme reflected the WEA curriculum for the 'informed citizen' – political economy, representative democracy, economics, history and international relations. Citizenship was at the core, which in itself accorded perfectly with the WEA's concern to contribute to post-war reconstruction at home and internationally.

It was the combination of war and the recognition that post-war alliances would best protect future peace and democracy that convinced the WEA to seize the initiative in establishing an international organisation. In 1943, the WEA's Annual Conference agreed to support the reconstruction of Workers' Education organisations in countries where they had been destroyed by fascism and war. This resolution, leaning heavily on the 1919 Greenwood Memorandum provided the basis for the 1945 conference which created the International Federation of Workers' Education Associations (IFWEA).

"Of course I know what I'm doing."

© Associated Newspapers

The optimism generated by the launch of IFWEA was well founded in the immediate post-war years. The WEA hosted the Secretariat in this formative period, and again in the 1980s. Common ground was secured with other organisations, principally in the Nordic countries, which represented quite different traditions. The most obvious of these were the organic links with their respective Social Democratic parties. The WEA recognised the potential difficulties, but believed a distinction could be maintained between formalising Party relationships (the non-WEA route) and supporting the basic values of mutuality, social justice and freedom of expression (the preferred WEA route). Over time, this notion of subscribing to a set of shared values emerged as the basis upon which IFWEA was to conduct its activities, and the WEA to participate in them.

But it was not long before international co-operation was severely tested. The break-up of the wartime alliance with the Soviet Union, the onset of the Cold War and the mistrust fuelled by McCarthyism severed any prospect of IFWEA achieving real purchase outside of Western and Northern Europe, North America and the Dominions.

The Cold War brought an end to international trade union unity and ushered in the emergence of competing 'Internationals', each defined ideologically. Trade union links were universally significant for Workers' Education and the fracture of trade union unity at international level caused many inter-union alliances to break down. Worse was to come – some unions were more than prepared to act as agents of their governments' foreign policy, particularly in relation to post-colonial Africa and Asia, and in Latin America.

All of this was to have a serious impact on workers' education and for the next 30 years the WEA's work with IFWEA was circumscribed by IFWEA's weaknesses. Its domestically-delivered international work concentrated on extending the international study visits programme, which had achieved some notable pre-war successes (the first WEA study visit was probably organised from Birmingham to Belgium in 1910). This was delivered primarily at District level, often as an extension of tutorial classes.

There were also reciprocal arrangements, again mostly at District level, where the WEA and a sister organisation would alternately host summer schools. Some of these were to become long-standing features of WEA activity, such as the Anglo-German summer school (Southern District) and the Nordic summer school (North Western District).

Many difficulties were in fact beyond the WEA's control – but there was also a lack of clarity and direction on the purpose of international work and how it could inform (and be informed by) domestic agendas. The development of the WEA into a National Association in 1991 finally created the framework for a coherent response to dramatic international change.

The fall of the Berlin Wall, the collapse of the old regimes in Central and Eastern Europe and the implosion of the Soviet Union undoubtedly created the stimulus to re-evaluate and re-launch the WEA's international programme in the 1990s. This process comprised three elements.

Firstly, the WEA was sensitive to organisational weaknesses in IFWEA and believed that it would be more effective if it developed a Regional structure. By 1991 the argument was won and the first of IFWEA's Regional bodies was established for Europe (EURO-WEA). In due course the

Secretariat of EURO-WEA was hosted by the WEA, followed by the establishment of a permanent WEA presence in Brussels.

Secondly, there were now numerous possibilities to create joint programmes between the WEA and its international partners, especially through activity designed to develop the capacity of Workers' Education organisations. This often led to concentrated support for improving tutor training, course design and management. During the 1990s bilateral support programmes were established with Workers' Education organisations in Hungary and Zambia, while multilateral activities spanned four continents in the development of international study circles.

Thirdly, new funding opportunities were available to help sustain development work. The WEA was remarkably successful in securing financial support from the mid-1990s – from the Department for International Development (DfID), formerly the Overseas Development Administration of the Foreign Office; the Community Fund, previously the National Lottery Charities Board; and from various programme streams of European Union funding.

Funders' confidence in the WEA to deliver high quality programmes

Plenary discussion at an IFWEA trade union seminar in Manchester, July 2002

fuelled its commitment to maintain and develop its internal capacity. For the first time, there was a real possibility of bringing the international programme in from the margins.

The historic problem for all Workers' Education organisations has been to ensure that international work is integrated into the life of the organisation. For membership organisations such as the WEA, this has required the active input of members in determining the direction and shape of the international programme. The argument for achieving convergence between the international and domestic programmes has been strengthened by the growing impact of globalisation, raising issues throughout the WEA curriculum.

The WEA's international work now draws on the spirit and meaning of Workers' Education as an international movement, where the respect for different traditions supports and sustains co-operation as an act of solidarity. As its Constitution now proclaims:

"The Association is committed to promoting and developing international awareness and co-operation in the educational process as a means of advancing human rights, sustainable development and civil society."

An international affairs class for disabled people at the Rockall Centre at Lavender Hill, south London

Seven | A Movement of Change, for Change
The Future of the WEA

The fall of the Berlin Wall in 1989 was the most visible symbol of a world transformed politically

The historical development of the WEA has been marked by its capacity to change with the times without compromising its vision and fundamental values. It has been resilient, flexible and responsive – qualities it will continue to need as it moves forward beyond 2003. It can do so with confidence and a realistic sense of optimism.

Much is already in place to meet the challenges ahead. There is a vibrant feel to its educational programme; demand over the five years from 1995 virtually doubled, from 6,000 courses to over 10,500, as enrolments expanded by 55%. Additional staffing and financial and technological support have been put in place to ensure that dramatic quantitative growth has been matched by qualitative development. For the programme as a whole, one of the most significant outcomes of the 1991 Constitutional agreement has been a framework where coherent processes and practices requiring action at National level sit alongside delegated powers reserved for Districts. External partnerships have been revitalised, especially at local and community levels, opening up major possibilities for programme development.

However, confidence and optimism must always be tempered by a sense of realism. Our working environment is likely to become much more competitive as new providers enter the field and current ones reinvent themselves to improve their competitive edge. New modes of delivery have the potential to undermine dramatically the most seminal partnership of all, that of the tutor and student.

Changes are underway at a fundamental level, which challenge the certainties we live by. Some appear almost abstract, such is their scale.

The increasing march of globalisation and corporate influence has changed the way we live

Far Left: Dyslexia can be a frustrating barrier to learning, and the WEA Northern District's Dyslexia Awareness courses have helped parents of dyslexic children encourage their innate creative talents

Left: Students and their children at a Birmingham Study Club, one of five in the city opened in 1999. Parents can pursue their studies while their children are looked after in a registered crèche

The rise of Corporate Power, in the words of eminent social scientist Jeffrey Harrod, has led to "the Global Retreat from Social Justice". Measured in the crudest of terms this meant that the difference in income between rich countries and poorer countries, which was 30 to 1 in 1960 and 60 to 1 in 1990, rose to 74 to 1 in 1997. We know also that the gulf within countries between the rich and poor is growing. The poor are getting poorer, migration from rural areas to urban areas and from poor countries to rich countries is growing, and pressures on political and social structures are mounting.

In Britain and other rich countries economies are being restructured, accompanied by the dismantling of traditional industries, the destruction of communities, internal migration, and tremendous pressures on infrastructure. Profound changes are taking place in the nature of employment as part-time and casual employment become commonplace, and temporary contracts and sub-contracting proliferate. Those at the bottom of the labour market, or at its margins, are the most vulnerable economically, socially and educationally.

Thus the re-definition of the working class continues. For the most vulnerable it is poverty which remains at its core and poverty manifests itself in multiple disadvantage. Low or inadequate income, fragile employment or unemployment, poor housing, and poor health and diet are the most obvious aspects. All too often this is accompanied by poverty of expectation and esteem, fuelled for many by 'failure' at school, and demonstrated through poor literacy and numeracy. Absent, in other words, are the 'skills for life'. This is the context in which the WEA has launched its major Basic Skills

The Women's Gardening Club at the Mill Hill and Edgware Branch learning about various aspects of horticulture in 2002. In recent years the Margaret James Fund has helped support the women's education development programme. Margaret James was a post-graduate student of R H Tawney at the London School of Economics, a lecturer at the University of Leicester and a member of the WEA East Midland District from 1937 until her death in 1943

initiative throughout England and Scotland, contemporary evidence of its historic commitment to Social Justice.

There is great opportunity for the WEA in the coming years to build upon the symmetry that exists between its vision and core values and those which underpin the struggle for Human Rights. The fundamental human right to education drives the WEA's commitment to inclusivity and our continuous efforts to reach those most disadvantaged in society.

But the future poses more complex challenges than the nature of the WEA's programme or the students it aims to reach. The WEA prides itself on being the largest voluntary provider of adult education in Britain but it never has been, and never should be, a provider alone. Through its membership base, it is a movement which throughout its history has campaigned on public policy issues, and its Constitution refers specifically to the objective of:

"Furthering the advancement of education to the end that all children, adolescents and adults may have full opportunities of the education needed for their complete individual and social development."

It made clear to the Government in 1998 that any notion of 'Lifelong Learning' needed to value in equal measure Learning for Economic Renewal, Learning for Social Cohesion, Learning for Cultural Renewal and Learning for Self-fulfilment.

Plurality in provision and in public funding has been at the heart of recent WEA campaigning because it believes passionately that without such an approach there never will be the step change in society that will allow Britain to claim it has achieved a culture of learning.

Through reasserting its campaigning role the WEA can affirm its distinctive character, develop its profile more widely, broaden the membership base and become a voice respected across a wide spectrum of public policy issues.

The future of the WEA?
A young boy gets to grips
with a WEA balloon at an
event in Maryhill in 1991

It is an intriguing characteristic of the Association that it is often more comfortable meeting external challenges than addressing internal issues. In the 1990s, for example, the WEA dramatically expanded and re-configured its programme, essential for survival under the prevailing external funding regime. But despite the achievements of the 1991 Constitutional arrangements, contentious structural and organisational questions remain unresolved. Although progress has been made there remain many unanswered elements to the question, 'How does the WEA build consistency and coherence within a framework responsive to locally identified need?'

Two of the most pressing tasks facing the WEA lie at the very heart of its organisational and educational presence. No description of the Association is adequate without reference to the role of voluntary members and tutors.

The WEA is a membership organisation composed of those who freely subscribe to its Charitable Aims and Purpose. It is from this source that so

At the Clovelly Centre in Southampton, the WEA's focus is on the route from education to employment. It runs accredited courses, often using Open College Network (OCN) qualifications, to help those from ethnic backgrounds overcome language and education barriers

West Mercia District has secured three-year lottery funding for a new health and fitness project targeting older Asian people in Dudley. The project is named *Tandrusti*, which means 'state of being free from illness'

much of the administrative and organisational strength of the movement stems, and from here that programme planning and recruitment is secured. Active voluntary members perform financial, publicity and class servicing roles. Critically, without them the fabric of representative democracy would be absent; there would be no governance deserving of the name.

With the new Membership Scheme operational since 2001, the WEA now has a platform for re-thinking the scope and nature of voluntarism. This poses many questions. Can the WEA accommodate volunteering roles for individuals outside of the membership framework, including the rights that membership conveys to participate in decision-making processes? Are the traditional structures that sustain voluntary members' involvement necessarily the most effective ways of supporting and encouraging voluntary activism?

Can the WEA extend the notion of voluntary members' rights, which are largely confined to representational matters, to embrace the notion of 'entitlement' to services, training and other forms of support? How can it

WEA Basic Skills programmes embrace courses designed for those whose mother tongue is not English. Here an ESOL group of students work together in the Midlands

ensure that its membership, including those who participate in the governance of the organisation, is representative of its student body as a whole? How can the 25% of all WEA students who come from the 2000 most disadvantaged neighbourhoods in England be successfully incorporated into the life of the WEA beyond the classroom?

For the WEA the process of 'volunteering' begins with the student who freely chooses to participate in educational activity. There is an important message here about the very nature of the learning process within the WEA. The individual's life experiences are valued, their enthusiasm for learning is acknowledged, and their collective participation in course activity creates 'added value' within the course and potentially, beyond into wider society. In 2001 a research study of students in two South Wales WEA Branches revealed a correlation between participation in the WEA and first time involvement in the community for those with no prior experience of community activism.

The role of the tutor is vital in this process. A deeply held belief in the value of students and tutors working together through the practical democracy of the 'negotiated' curriculum remains a guiding principle of the WEA. A true understanding of the WEA's curriculum can only be appreciated if it is acknowledged that 'subject' and 'student' cannot be separated.

Yet there is now a very real risk that the role of the tutor, as traditionally defined and valued, is under threat, weakening the ability of students to exercise control over their own learning process. As public trust in 'professionalism' is lost and notions of public accountability are distorted, so professional independence and integrity risk being undermined. In the 2002 BBC Reith Lectures the philosopher Onora O'Neill put the issue quite bluntly:

"If we want a culture of public service, professionals and public servants must be free to serve the public rather than their paymasters."

In relation to the tutor's role, what is being suggested here is that if we rightly demand professionalism, we must concede autonomy.

Professor Lindsay Paterson of the Moray House Institute of Education, University of Edinburgh, giving the keynote address to the WEA Scotland Millenium Celebration Conference in Glasgow, 2002

This is potentially the most important task for the WEA in the coming years, and it will have to be achieved within an environment that demands more evidence than ever of our institutional 'accountability to paymasters'. The task ahead is to protect the space that recognises the integrity and professionalism of our tutors and the distinctiveness of their relationship with students individually and collectively. It implies that the WEA's various systems and procedures, whilst acknowledging our commitment to proper levels of public accountability, are designed primarily to facilitate the way we deliver teaching and learning.

This is no small task for an organisation that is so often disparate and confusing to the outside world. Yet the WEA across 100 years has been and remains at the heart of Britain's cultural and democratic traditions. Our past and present achievements should serve as an inspiration for the future, allowing us to address with confidence the educational needs of tomorrow's adult students.

Appendices

One of the WEA's major partners in Asia is the Self-Employed
Women's Association of India (SEWA). Delegates at SEWA's 2002
conference in Ahmedabad celebrate the organisation's remarkable
growth in recent years

Acknowledgements

Many colleagues within the WEA and beyond have made a valuable contribution to this publication. Drafts of individual sections were improved through the advice of John Atkins, Colin Thorne, Dave Spooner, Marian Young and Robert Lochrie. Early reading of the manuscript as a whole was provided by Julia Jones, Stephen Roberts and Peter Templeton, each of whom offered valuable guidance on the direction and balance of the text. Additional research at the WEA National Archive was undertaken by Graham Marsh. Editorial guidance was generously forthcoming from Irene Reed and Ros Carr at Frameworks. Picture research was undertaken by Maria Catt, Halina Hassett, Joyce Connon, Donna McDermott and Ros Carr. Vanessa Lai and Arron Wakeling of Frameworks designed and produced this publication.

For picture assistance many thanks to Phil Dunn at the People's History Museum in Manchester, Gillian Lonergan at the Co-operative College, Christine Coates, Librarian of the WEA Archives at London Metropolitan University, and Kate Bradley, Librarian at Toynbee Hall.

Mel Doyle, January 2003

Chronology

1903
- WEA founded as 'The Association to Promote the Higher Education of Working Men', becoming the 'Workers Educational Association' in 1905
- WEA founder Albert Mansbridge elected Honorary Secretary, and from 1906 full-time General Secretary
- First WEA National Delegate Conference held at Toynbee Hall, London

1904
- First WEA Branch established at Reading

1905
- 1000 people attend the 1905 National Delegate Conference in Birmingham

1907
- Oxford Conference on 'Oxford and Working Class Education'
- WEA Working Party on the Education of Women formed
- Adoption of first WEA Constitution
- First Districts functioning in the North West and the Midlands

1908
- First tutorial classes organised in Rochdale and Longton
- Oxford Conference Report published, leading to Government funding for the WEA
- Joint Committee of Oxford and the WEA organised on a permanent basis
- William Temple elected first President of the WEA
- First issue of *The Highway* published

1909
- Central Joint Advisory Committee of the WEA and the Universities established
- Ruskin College 'Strike' and creation of the Central Labour College

1910
- First WEA Summer School at Oxford

1912
- WEA Central Library established at Toynbee Hall

1913
- Eight Districts organised within England
- Mansbridge in Australia, leading to the progressive establishment of WEAs in the Dominions

1915
- Mansbridge resigns as General Secretary through ill health, and J M Mactavish is appointed his successor
- Constitutional change explicitly grants delegated powers to Districts
- First WEA Study Guides published

1917
- WEA joins the lobby for post-war Education reform, leading to the 1918 Education Act

1919
- 219 Branches in existence
- Scottish District Council established
- Final Report of the Adult Education Committee of the Ministry of Reconstruction
- Workers' Education Trade Union Committee formed
- Greenwood 'Memorandum' on the WEA and international activities published
- First woman tutor organiser appointed

1922
- WEA demonstrates against 'Geddes Cuts' in public expenditure

1924
- Government grants 'Responsible Body' status to Districts in England, 16 Districts functioning
- International Conference on Labour Education held in Oxford

1925
- Failure of TUC initiative to bring WETUC and the National Council of Labour Colleges together

1928
- R H Tawney succeeds Temple as President of the WEA, and holds the position until 1944

1934
- WEA 'Sixpenny Library' launched
- First WEA/International Labour Organisation Summer School held in Geneva

1936
- WEA appoints Youth Officers for work with the 18-25s

1939
- 635 Branches and 290 Student groups operating across the WEA
- WETUC affiliations rise to 27 trade unions
- Circulation of *The Highway* reaches 20,000

1941
- Programme of courses for Civil Defence workers introduced

1942
- R A Butler issues guiding principles for state funding of voluntary associations
- WEA along with the NUT enters the campaign for a new post-war Education Act, enacted in 1944
- WEA tutors past and present help deliver the Army Education Corps' 'British Way and Purpose' programme

1945
- Army Council formally acknowledges the WEA as 'a vital partner'
- Election of a Labour Government: 14 Ministers have a background in the WEA
- Government grant regulations relaxed, henceforth grant related to overall size of Districts' programmes

- London Conference leads to the formation of the International Federation of Workers' Education Associations

1952

- Albert Mansbridge dies

1954

- Report of the Ashby Committee on the Organisation and Finance of Adult Education
- Pilot Areas Scheme in trade union education introduced

1963

- WETUC and NCLC integrated into new TUC Regional Education scheme

1966

- National Delegate Conference introduces an 'opt out' membership scheme

1969

- Publication of *Unfinished Business*

1973

- Report of the Russell Committee on Adult Education

1975

- Report of the Alexander Committee on Adult Education in Scotland

1976

- £100,000 made available by Government to support WEA delivery of the 'Russell Priorities'

1983

- Government claws back Districts 'surpluses' and imposes 8.3% cut in grant

1988

- End of 'Responsible Body' status

1989

- Government invites WEA to consider possibility of receiving grant via Local Authorities
- First 'Return to Learn' programme delivered

1991

- National Delegate Conference agrees an 'integrated' Constitution, Welsh and Northern Ireland Districts withdraw from the National Association
- EURO-WEA created as the first Regional body of IFWEA

1992

- Further and Higher Education Act passed, Further Education Funding Council created

1999

- WEA sustains 1,600 partnerships with other organisations and bodies at local and regional levels

2000

- Learning and Skills Act passed, Learning and Skills Council formed
- National Delegate Conference agrees an 'opt in' membership scheme, returning to the pre-1966 position

Bibliography

Albert Mansbridge, *An Adventure in Working Class Education,* 1920*

T W Price, *The Story of the Workers' Educational Association, 1903-24,* 1924*

A J Corfield, *Epoch in Workers' Education: A History of the Workers' Educational Association Trade Union Committee,* 1969*

Bernard Jennings, *Knowledge is Power: A Short History of the Workers' Educational Association, 1903-1978,* 1979*

John Atkins, *Neither Crumbs nor Condescension: The Central Labour College, 1909-15,* 1981*

John Holford, *Union Education in Britain – A TUC Activity,* 1994 (Dept of Adult Education, University of Nottingham)

Lawrence Goldman, *Dons and Workers: Oxford and Adult Education since 1850,* 1995 (OUP)

Roger Fieldhouse, *A History of Modern British Adult Education,* 1996 (NIACE)

Jonathan Rose, *The Intellectual Life of the British Working Class,* 2001 (Yale University Press)

Bernard Jennings, *Albert Mansbridge – The Life and Work of the Founder of the WEA,* 2002
(University of Leeds/WEA – Leeds Studies in Continuing Education Series)

Stephen Roberts (ed.), *A Ministry of Enthusiasm: Centenary Essays on the WEA,* 2003 (Pluto)

The WEA National Archive, housed at the London Metropolitan University, provides a valuable source of material on the WEA. Minute books, correspondence, personal papers, series pamphlets, Conference and Annual Reports, and a host of other documentation is available.

For further information and to make an appointment to visit the archive, please contact:
Christine Coates, London Metropolitan University, WEA National Archive, Learning Centre, 236-250 Holloway Road, London, N7 6PP Tel: 020 7753 3184 Fax: 020 7753 3191 or email: c.coates@unl.ac.uk

* Copies of these books are available in the WEA National Archive, London Metropolitan University
   for reading purposes only. No loan service is available